GUIDED MEDITATION

The Complete Guide Against Sleep Disorders

(Guided Meditations for Self-healing and Stress Management)

Martin Sparks

Published by Alex Howard

Martin Sparks

All Rights Reserved

Guided Meditation: The Complete Guide Against Sleep Disorders (Guided Meditations for Self-healing and Stress Management)

ISBN 978-1-77485-070-1

All rights reserved. No part of this guide may be reproduced in any form without permission in writing from the publisher except in the case of brief quotations embodied in critical articles or reviews.

Legal & Disclaimer

The information contained in this book is not designed to replace or take the place of any form of medicine or professional medical advice. The information in this book has been provided for educational and entertainment purposes only.

The information contained in this book has been compiled from sources deemed reliable, and it is accurate to the best of the Author's knowledge; however, the Author cannot guarantee its accuracy and validity and cannot be held liable for any errors or omissions. Changes are periodically made to this book. You must consult your doctor or get professional medical advice before using any of the suggested remedies, techniques, or information in this book.

Upon using the information contained in this book, you agree to hold harmless the Author from and against any damages, costs, and expenses, including any legal fees potentially resulting from the application of any of the information provided by this guide. This disclaimer applies to any damages or injury caused by the use and application, whether directly or indirectly, of any advice or information presented, whether for breach of contract, tort, negligence, personal injury, criminal intent, or under any other cause of action.

You agree to accept all risks of using the information presented inside this book. You need to consult a professional medical practitioner in order to ensure you are both able and healthy enough to participate in this program.

Table of Contents

INTRODUCTION 1

CHAPTER 1: THE BODY SCAN 3

CHAPTER 2: THE SIGNIFICANCE OF USING MEDITATION TO IMPROVE PROBLEM SOLVING SKILLS 13

CHAPTER 3: WHAT KEEPS PEOPLE UP AT NIGHT? 26

CHAPTER 4: YOUR THOUGHTS DO NOT DEFINE YOU 35

CHAPTER 5: GUIDED MEDITATION TO PREVENT PANIC ATTACKS AND TO MANAGE THEM 46

CHAPTER 6: MANIFEST YOUR IDEAL WORKDAY IN FIVE MINUTES | 5 MINUTES | 342 WORDS 73

CHAPTER 7: THE WHITE HORSE 77

CHAPTER 8: FIRST WEEK OF MEDITATIONS 84

CHAPTER 10: DEEPENING 128

CHAPTER 11: ILLUSTRATION OF MEDITATION POINTS... 138

CHAPTER 12: BENEFITS OF MEDITATION 158

CHAPTER 13: INTRODUCTION TO MEDITATION 175

CONCLUSION 183

Introduction

This book covers the topic of Importance of Meditation, Law of Cause and Effect, Developing Mindfulness-Based Cognitive Therapy, Acceptance and Compromise and more.

This book will teach you Relaxation Techniques for Anxiety, how to master Breathing for Relaxation, Jacobson's Progressive Relaxation Technique, Meditation for Heart and Kindness and Self-Compassion.

At the completion of this book you will have a good understanding of how to meditate and you be able to do that even if you never meditated before.

Once again, thanks for downloading this book, I hope you find it to be helpful!

One thing that we may notice over time in our lives is that stress is a very controlling factor in how we respond to the different stimuli in life. For example, have you ever had a situation where you wish you could respond to it better, but stress just overtakes your thought process? Do you feel like your anxiety is the one in control at times?

If that is the case, then let this book help you.

Here, we'll talk about meditation, its role in treating anxiety and how it can change your life. Lots of times, people don't realize how helpful meditation is, and how a little goes a long way. But we'll tap into that in this helpful book, and not only that, we'll give you invaluable tips to help you meditate better. By the end of this book, you'll know how to meditate for success, and in turn, be able to live a better, less stressful existence, which is something that we all should be working towards, right? I think so, and here, we'll help you learn valuable techniques that can help with eliminating stress in its tracks.

Chapter 1: The Body Scan

This first meditation is called Body Scan and it is one of the most famous beginners technique that are thought in some of the best in person courses out there. It is also the first technique we teach our students during our live seminars, so it is the perfect place to start if you are completely new to this world. It will be also used during the other two meditations in this book, so we highly suggest you to start from here and not skip it, especially if you have never done that.

The Body Scan allows you to reach a deep sense of calmness and relaxation inside your body using your directed attention and breath.

Following my voice, you will start to direct your focus on each part of your body, painting a clear picture of it inside your mind. This simple exercise will relieve a lot of stress and anxiety, as it grounds yourself in your very own body.

Let's get started.

Find a comfortable, relaxed and balanced position. Give yourself permission to be completely present for yourself, and let your body and mind calm down until they become soft and relaxed.

Breathe in, feel relaxed...
breathe out, feel calm...
Breathe in, feel relaxed...
breathe out, feel calm...
Breathe in, feel relaxed...
breathe out, feel calm...
Breathe in, feel relaxed...
breathe out, feel calm...

Allow the mind to distance itself from all thoughts and orientate awareness on your breath. Breathe naturally and do not force a specific rhythm. Let your breath come and go.

Carefully, now, drive your attention from the breath to the space in which you are.

Feel the energy and atmosphere of this space as it permeates all of your being. Notice the noises in the background. Maybe there is a clock ticking, maybe there are cars passing just outside your

windows. Whatever you feel it is fine, let your attention rest on the external.
Breathe in, feel relaxed...
breathe out, feel calm...
Breathe in, feel relaxed...
breathe out, feel calm...
Breathe in, feel relaxed...
breathe out, feel calm...
Breathe in, feel relaxed...
breathe out, feel calm...
Now bring the attention back to the breath. Take your time and you will naturally reach a place of warmth and ease. Stay in this state where you feel your body and mind completely calm, relaxed and full of peace for a few minutes, without letting go the focus on your breath.
Breathe in, feel relaxed...
breathe out, feel calm...
Breathe in, feel relaxed...
breathe out, feel calm...
Breathe in, feel relaxed...
breathe out, feel calm...
Breathe in, feel relaxed...
breathe out, feel calm...

Breathe in, feel relaxed...
breathe out, feel calm...
Breathe in, feel relaxed...
breathe out, feel calm...
Breathe in, feel relaxed...
breathe out, feel calm...
Breathe in, feel relaxed...
breathe out, feel calm...

Now, begin to scan your body from the bottom of your toes up to the top of your head. Do this slowly and stop on each part of your body to listen to what it has to tell you. If you feel contracted on a specific area, keep the attention on that part for as long as you feel it relaxing. It is important that you do not force this process, just keep breathing and you will feel your body getting more and more relaxed.

Begin from your big toes, how do they feel today? Have you ever asked yourself this question? Pain a clear picture of them inside your head, as you slowly shift your attention to your ankles.

During this practice, each joint is a crucial point where anxiety can infiltrate itself. If you find a part of your body that feels

tight, you can softly massage it with your hands until you feel it completely relaxed.
Breathe in, feel relaxed...
breathe out, feel calm...
Breathe in, feel relaxed...
breathe out, feel calm...
Breathe in, feel relaxed...
breathe out, feel calm...
Breathe in, feel relaxed...
breathe out, feel calm...
Reach your knees and feel them. How are your knees today? Maybe they are sore because you have been standing all day or made an effort yesterday. Maybe they are relaxed and strong. Whatever you feel, it is okay. Moving up your quadriceps, reach your pelvic floor and genital area.

This is an extremely crucial zone of your body when it comes to anxiety and stress, as a lot of energy is drawn down to it by your neuromuscular system. Spend a few minutes on your pelvic, before moving upwards. I will give you the time you need.
Breathe in, feel relaxed...
breathe out, feel calm...
Breathe in, feel relaxed...

breathe out, feel calm...
Breathe in, feel relaxed...
breathe out, feel calm...
Breathe in, feel relaxed...
breathe out, feel calm...
Breathe in, feel relaxed...
breathe out, feel calm...
Breathe in, feel relaxed...
breathe out, feel calm...
Breathe in, feel relaxed...
breathe out, feel calm...
Breathe in, feel relaxed...
breathe out, feel calm...
Breathe in, feel relaxed...
breathe out, feel calm...
Breathe in, feel relaxed...
breathe out, feel calm...
Breathe in, feel relaxed...
breathe out, feel calm...
Breathe in, feel relaxed...
breathe out, feel calm...

Keep going up, reaching your chest and your shoulders. This is where a lot of tension can be usually found, so take your time in this area. If you feel a bit stiff, do not hesitate to move your arms, until they

reach a comfortable position. Feel your lungs and heart, still beating strong even if you had a rough day or are facing issues at the moment.
The heart keeps beating, the lungs keep breathing.
Breathe in, feel relaxed...
breathe out, feel calm...
Breathe in, feel relaxed...
breathe out, feel calm...
Breathe in, feel relaxed...
breathe out, feel calm...
Breathe in, feel relaxed...
breathe out, feel calm...
Breathe in, feel relaxed...
breathe out, feel calm...
Breathe in, feel relaxed...
breathe out, feel calm...
Breathe in, feel relaxed...
breathe out, feel calm...
Breathe in, feel relaxed...
breathe out, feel calm...
And finally you reach your head. Keep breathing into your head and feel the air slowly filling every empty space of your head.

How does the air feel? Is it cold or warm? What does it smell like? Do you like it? Those are all simple questions that we forget to ask ourself during the day, but that can help us ground ourself back into our body.
Breathe in, feel relaxed...
breathe out, feel calm...
Breathe in, feel relaxed...
breathe out, feel calm...
Breathe in, feel relaxed...
breathe out, feel calm...
Breathe in, feel relaxed...
breathe out, feel calm...
Stay in this beautiful space for as long as you want, you deserve it.
Breathe in, feel relaxed...
breathe out, feel calm...
Breathe in, feel relaxed...
breathe out, feel calm...
Breathe in, feel relaxed...
breathe out, feel calm...
Breathe in, feel relaxed...
breathe out, feel calm...
Breathe in, feel relaxed...
breathe out, feel calm...

Breathe in, feel relaxed...
breathe out, feel calm...
Breathe in, feel relaxed...
breathe out, feel calm...
Breathe in, feel relaxed...
breathe out, feel calm...
Breathe in, feel relaxed...
breathe out, feel calm...
Breathe in, feel relaxed...
breathe out, feel calm...
Breathe in, feel relaxed...
breathe out, feel calm...
Breathe in, feel relaxed...
breathe out, feel calm...
Breathe in, feel relaxed...
breathe out, feel calm...
Breathe in, feel relaxed...
breathe out, feel calm...
Breathe in, feel relaxed...
breathe out, feel calm...
Breathe in, feel relaxed...
breathe out, feel calm...
Now bring the attention back to the body and start feeling your arms and legs once again. You can close your hands or move

your fingers, just to take control of the space around you.

Please, keep the eyes closed for now and enjoy the beautiful moment you are living. You have given yourself the time to feel better and that is absolutely incredible.

Breathe in, feel relaxed...
breathe out, feel calm...
Breathe in, feel relaxed...
breathe out, feel calm...
Breathe in, feel relaxed...
breathe out, feel calm...
Breathe in, feel relaxed...
breathe out, feel calm...

Now become aware of the environment around you once again. Feel the different sounds, the temperature of the room you are in and once you are ready, open the eyes again.

Chapter 2: The Significance Of Using Meditation To Improve Problem Solving Skills

The minds of human beings constantly engage in different forms of dialogue. They are internal debates that are related to the emotional and meaningful associations where one thought is triggered by the other. For instance, when we hear some piece of music, the mind immediately begins to wander and find out the previous time that we had the same music. It thus relates to a particular incident such as how a relationship did not work out. Holding on to such negative emotions and feelings may result in the veering off of the mind to a state that is filled with self pity, worries about what the future has to hold and criticisms.

It is as a result of this that most individuals find it necessary to get involved in the activities that involve meditation from time to time. The main reason is to enjoy the numerous benefits that come with the practice. The activity has been found to eliminate any chances of stress and replace it with huge amounts of inner peace. It is a very vital tool that is used in the balancing of emotions, assist people to handle their psychological and physical stress and provide a high level of peace at any particular moment. There are many techniques that are employed during the meditation process. They are encouraged to help the individual involved to explore some of the difficult emotions and feelings in a direct way. They may be in the type of individual or guided processes. Although most of the meditation processes are performed individually, it can be tough. In such cases, it is essential to get a teacher or a guide to take you through the process successfully.

Guided meditation

You can take part in guided meditation since it requires a lot of effort for an individual to meditate as an individual. For this reason, there is the guided meditation, which enables you to go through the process of meditation in a successful way. It helps you to reach the state of peace and calm that you desire. This is achieved by taking each step at a time and has been found to be the greatest gift that an individual can receive through meditation. Some of the other benefits include a deep sense of great joy and happiness.

Types of meditation

The different types of meditation can range between five minutes and one hour to complete. These help you to focus on the particular aspect of life with which you deserve peace. It may be an item that has bothered you for a long time. The following are some of the meditations that you can perform to attain calm:

• Meditation to awaken abundance is done through the use of breath, attention, and intention to bring about the connection to the abundance that is richly flowing.

• Meditation to help you work on your wanderlust deviates most of the thoughts that are directed towards the most external world. It brings this energy into the nose, mouth and eyes to provide sensory nourishment.

• Healing meditation helps people to be in touch with their bodies and have a connection with their emotions. With this, you are able to return to a state that is most perfect, divine and pure. It is thus the greatest journey towards wholeness.

• Meditation to make you get the summer love. It acts as a journey to the center and the deepest part of creation. This is the place that carries a special meaning for individuals.

• The meditation that helps you to obtain perfect health. Stress usually occurs when most of your needs are not met. This can be changed with a particular level of awareness, and attentiveness.

• The meditation that helps you to stop the desire to control. It focuses on the part that offers the thought that we are in control of things. It explores the areas where has the fear of the unknown and craves the need for certainty.

- Meditation to help you build your creativity. It helps to harness the power that comes with coincidence
- Dream meditation helps the individual to connect to the most divine element of self by bringing the state of waking into the dream state.
- Meditation to help release emotions
- Gratitude meditation
- Meditation on global peace
- Meditation to let go of pain
- Meditations that help you follow through your commitments
- Meditation for empowerment.
- Inner fire guided meditation
- Meditation for third Chakra

Where to find the guided meditation

A number of experts offer guidelines that you can use to conduct the most relaxing meditation process in different forms. These include physical classes, recorded audio messages, and video links and phone conversations. You can now get an introduction to mindfulness meditation that you can easily perform on your own. These are audio and visual instructions

that are provided on the internet and give you the opportunities to play once you have turned on your speakers. There are varied benefits of meditation: Some of the most common kinds of meditations guidelines that they offer include:
• Breathing meditation
• Complete meditation instructions
• Breath, body sound meditation
• Loving kindness meditation
• The meditation that helps you work with difficulties
• Body scan meditation
• Sound and body meditation
• Body scans used for sleep

All of these are able to lead you through a journey that helps you relax in a deep way as they take you into a secret garden. In this, you are able to think about any issue of your choice.

On the other hand, you can also choose to take part in the practice of loving kindness meditation, which is done once every month. It is conducted over the phone and takes 30 minutes to complete. It happens in the form of a teleconference that offers a convenient and effective way of meditation. This helps to bring about change in the form of a positive attitude. It is in the way that it enhances the quality with which love and acceptance towards you and other people can be cultivated in a systematic way. It enables you to send invitations in the form of well wishes to yourself. Thus, it helps to alleviate the feeling of distress that you may possess. However, it is not meant to suppress the feelings as they tend to occur, but is expected to soothe and heal the wound in the gentlest way as you enjoy the comfort of your home or your office.

Reasons why you should engage in meditation

Meditation is a regularly performed exercise based on the number of positive aspects that it offers to the body. The following are some of the benefits of guided meditation:

• It has been shown that Meditation Improves Your Creativity and Problem-Solving Skills

The minds of people can be compared to racing cars. They are always in the constant process of thinking. The same thoughts that people had yesterday are the same ones that they have today and will have tomorrow. Thus, they keep going round every week, months and year. With this, more often than not, people are stuck in the same thoughts that keep repeating themselves in their brains. In turn, there is very little room and space that is left to obtain new ideas. The meditation process brings about a new element of flow through which all things will be getting in a natural way. You will not need to struggle and force things to take place. You will involve yourself in fewer activities that on the other hand will help you to make more accomplishments. It is because your mind will be in a better position to receive many insights in the form of flashes and fresh perspectives.

• It reduces the chances of burnout and the levels of stress

If stress is not managed in a proper manner it can turn chronic and thus lead to faster aging and enhance your ability to become sick. In this case, there is an increased chance of an individual with prolonged stress to acquire a high number of disorders and illnesses. The body gets the chance to relieve stress through meditation. In addition, it reduces the effects of the fight or flight that people have during times of danger or during battle. Besides this, stress is generated from almost all activities and experiences of life. These include traffic jams, disagreement with others or criticisms. Through regular meditation, you can dissipate built up stress and maintain a high level of alertness and restfulness.

• Meditation helps you to maintain relationships that are Harmonious

A meditation that is done on a regular basis helps you to obtain the ability to be available for a co-worker or a loved one. This is in the way that it makes people listen to what others are saying or their needs in a better way. It provides the possibility to handle situations in a more objective way, realize when you are likely to be triggered and select the most appropriate way to respond in a conscious way. It is easier to respond as opposed to react when one is in a position that is well centered and balanced. One of the things that are highly valued and important in a relationship is the full presence and awareness of an individual.

- Meditation gives you better memory, concentration and a good ability to learn

It has been discovered that the ability of an individual to explore the deepest potential of their brain is through meditation. This is in relation to their ability to adapt, focus and learn. Meditation is an exceptional tool that awakens the connections between neurons in the brain and provides the ability to reduce stress patterns that keep reoccurring. As such, the individual is able to remain as focused as possible.

- Meditation reduces the chances of insomnia, depression and anxiety

There are profound benefits that come from the decision to sit quietly and explore within. It is a result of the ability of the brain to release several helpful chemicals. These include dopamine, endorphins, serotonin and oxytocins. Each of these chemicals plays a significant role in increasing happiness. They also bring about feelings of calm, security and contentment. At the same time, they minimize the feelings of fear and anxiety as much as possible. According to research, engaging in meditation is a great benefit to individuals who are experiencing chronic pain, thus helping them to reduce the need for meditation in a significant way.

• It improves the immunity function

The relaxation of the brain during meditation has been found to greatly enhance the flow of blood to different parts of the body. This is one of the very important steps through which the immune functions in the body are improved and the chances of disease attacks reduced.

Some of the other healing benefits of guided meditation include:

- The decreased level of hypertension and blood pressure
- Reduced levels of cholesterol
- An increased use of oxygen in the body
- Decreased portions of hormones such as cortisol and adrenaline that bring about stress
- An elevated production of DHEA, which is an anti aging hormone
- Reduced level of insomnia, depression and anxiety.

There is no way that an individual can focus in constructive thoughts with a mind that is completely filled with worries. This is why people need to sit still and maintain silence on a regular basis. Since Meditation Improves Your Creativity and Problem-Solving Skills it is important that you engage in effective guided meditation. It also helps you to improve your memory, make informed decisions and increase your attention span. In this case, the more times that you practice meditation, the more you are able to make better decisions. Find a reputable site that offers guided meditation and make an attempt to use them as soon as possible. They will help you to focus on a particular chosen theme of the day and give you utmost peace and calm. You can begin with the meditative process that makes use of the meditative belly breathing as it will help you to increase your concentration. Indeeed, it can plausibly be argued that the significance of meditation cannot be overlooked under any circumstances. It is a great way of improving one's problem solving skills and the general thinking.

Chapter 3: What Keeps People Up At Night?

On the off chance that you're similar to me, at that point, you presumably go through numerous a late evening lying alert like a type of animation character. You know, the ones who can't rest and lie there with ragged looking eyes? It's not how I'd prefer to go through the night, however once in a while, it just feels like everything is keeping me wakeful.

Possibly it's a trickling spigot, or the noisy neighbours, or the sounds from the road. Whatever it is, seemingly insignificant details like these out of nowhere appear to be additional irritating at 2 a.m. On the off chance that this has ever transpired, at that point you realize how baffling it feels, and how rapidly the morning comes when you despite everything haven't gotten any rest.

It can feel like you're the just one wakeful on the planet, however you're certainly not. These sorts of issues are the situation for around 50 to 70 million Americans, as indicated by the CDC. That is a great deal of gazing at the roof or tallying acknowledged sheep.

Rest issues may not appear too enormous of an arrangement, particularly since 70 million of us are strolling around tired and nothing really awful appears to occur. So it may be stunning to hear that lack of sleep can prompt essentially every issue under the sun. Alright, perhaps only one out of every odd issue. Be that as it may, it is connected to a great deal of things, for example, hypertension, diabetes, sadness, and weight, just as types of malignant growth, expanded mortality, and diminished personal satisfaction and efficiency, as per the CDC.

It's alarming stuff, thus unquestionably worth fixing. We should begin with this rundown of potential reasons you may be remaining up throughout the night, and afterward go from that point.

1. That Late Cup Of Coffee

In the event that you spend the entire evening hurling and turning however don't generally have the foggiest idea why, recollect how much caffeine you swallowed for the duration of the day. Did you have a 4 p.m. mug of espresso to get past that last hour of work? Or then again perhaps a couple of cups of tea before bed?

Regardless of whether you're ready to nod off around evening time, that caffeine can in any case make it difficult to get a decent night's rest. As Bernadette Farrell noted HuffingtonPost.com, "Specialists at Harvard Medical School report that caffeine squares adenosine, your body's characteristic rest inciting operator ... [caffeine also] breaks your rest, with the goal that you wake up more frequently during the night."

This is certainly something to consider, particularly since it takes a stunning four to seven hours for caffeine to leave the body, as indicated by Farrell. So in the event that you can't rest, consider avoiding your evening and late night espressos. Or possibly change to decaf.

2. You're In Pain

A beating cerebral pain or a firm back may be the purpose behind your late-night inconveniences. As indicated by an article on Health, "In one investigation, 15 percent of Americans detailed experiencing constant torment, and 66% additionally revealed having rest issues. Back torment, cerebral pains, and temporomandibular joint condition (issues with the jaw muscles) are the fundamental driver of torment related rest misfortune." On the off chance that you figure agony may be your concern, at that point I suggest hitting up a warm shower before bed, or laying down with a warming cushion, as it can help loosen up your muscles. On the off chance that that doesn't push, at that point converse with your primary care physician about what may be going on.

3. Your Room Isn't The Right Temp

I for one love resting in a freezing cold room. There's only something about cuddling into the sheets that feels so right. But, on the off chance that my sweeping tumbles off in the night, overlook it — I wake up in a split second and can't return to rest.

So it appears to be fairly clear that a virus room (or a very hot one) can wreck your night. As Sarah Klein noted on HuffingtonPost.com, "You may think you recognize what makes for a comfortable room, however there's real research analyzing ideal dozing temperature. For the most part, the sweet spot is somewhere close to 60 and 67 degrees Fahrenheit ... with temps beneath 54 or over 75 regarded problematic to your sleep."

4. The entirety Of That Stress

We've all lain wakeful around evening time pondering work, our relationship, or that unbalanced thing we said in second grade. Call it stress, call it tension, call it terrible cherished recollections. Whatever it will be, it's actual the psyche has an astonishing method of keeping us up around evening time.

The most noticeably awful part, however, is when contemplations winding wild. As Alan Henry called attention to on

Lifehacker.com, "The more you chase after your musings around and around, the more profound that criticism circle of pressure and uneasiness goes." Yup, practically.

So do whatever you can do to reign in your contemplations, be it with reflection, yoga, or perusing a book. Essentially, do whatever will assist you with slowing down and turn off that cerebrum of yours.

5. Your Late-Night Sugary Snacks

I don't think about you, however I love a late night bite, or two, or three. Ordinarily, the sweet the better. What's more, know I'm not the only one. As Alessandra Bulow brought up on Epicurious.com, individuals regularly go to comfort nourishments as an approach to slow down.

In any case, shockingly, anyway delectable, sweet tidbits won't help you rest. That is on the grounds that they cause glucose changes, which make it hard to rest, Bulow noted. So either skirt your evening doughnut, or include a few nourishments with protein and fat to help balance things out and forestall a glucose crash.

6. Nodding off With Your Phone

Incredibly, nodding off with telephone close by isn't the most ideal approach to rest (particularly when you incidentally drop it all over.) Not just is it a tremendous interruption that doesn't permit your cerebrum to kill, however it additionally has a method of placing your psyche into overdrive.

As per Heather Hatfield on WebMD.com, "As your cerebrum fires up, its electrical action increments and neurons begin to race — the specific inverse of what ought to occur before rest ... The physical demonstration of reacting to a computer game or even an email makes your body tense ... as you get focused on, your body can go into a 'battle or flight' reaction, and accordingly, cortisol, a pressure hormone delivered by the adrenal organ, is discharged, making a circumstance barely helpful for rest." Do yourself some help and leave your telephone in another room while you rest, or if nothing else far off.

7. You Aren't Wearing Socks

A few people loathe staying in bed socks since they're bothersome or hot. They additionally get parts in the sheets, and it can turn out to be a remarkable torment. I for one attempt to hit the sack with socks on, yet wake up with them mysteriously absent. (It's most likely my body dismissing them in the night.)

But then, anyway hot or awkward it might sound, laying down with socks on should be an extraordinary method to manage your internal heat level, which as we probably am aware is significant for acceptable rest. As per Klein, "Regardless of whether you've set the indoor regulator effectively, a few people are simply arranged to having colder than agreeable limits. Be that as it may, this can turn into an issue at sleep time, since warm hands and feet are a piece of a fragile thermoregulatory move that appears to foresee how rapidly you'll nod off, as indicated by a recent report." Slip into certain socks

Rest is a whimsical thing, so don't give it any motivations to forsake you in the night. Keep an eye on your caffeine utilization, telephone use, and room temp, and ideally you'll show signs of improvement night's rest.

Chapter 4: Your Thoughts Do Not Define You

We start trying to figure out the world around us from the moment we have consciousness: where to get food, how to get love, and how to feel healthy. As we whiz through our formative years, we are being trained to think "faster," "deeper," and "harder" to solve life problems. Around the time we are adults, the majority of us have a co-dependent relationship with our minds, in which our emotions have so much control over our world. We come to believe our thoughts are real, and they describe us. Meditation helps us to untangle this relationship.

A BUSY MIND

Whether we notice it or not, our minds are continually whirring away, trying to make sense of complex emotions, creating order, and getting approval and praise from others, or running through entirely made-up scenarios and obsessively worrying about them. As this sequence carries on, we fly through every passing moment, totally missing the fact that it is the only moment we actually live in, that every moment is profoundly rich in sensation and space, and calm and insight. We sometimes miss out on the joy of living in our bodies by living in our minds, feeling what it feels like to be alive at this moment, right now. Meditation helps us to recognize that our thoughts are creations of our brains, that we can be objectively observing them, and that we can choose how they affect us.

MEDITATION IS NOT...

You may have some images in your head about what meditation looks like, who can do it, and about what it all is. I urge you to discard any preconceptions about meditation that you have. (I will not ask you to try and levitate).

You don't need to be some kind of person, wear any particular type of clothing, travel to the Himalayas, chant, or pray to meditate. You just have to give yourself the suggested time for each practice, and then follow the process. Meditation is important, so it's not going to hurt you. Your day-to-day experience can differ, from practice to practice. Some days or workouts will feel great, and some will feel like a fierce war. But if you stick to it, you can find a path to relaxation, tranquility, and peace that you may not have traveled before, and it can become one that you greatly value.

EMBRACE THE PRESENT MOMENT

Meditation is the practice of calming your thoughts to become fully conscious of the present moment. You will live in it more fully, with growing consciousness, more profound responsiveness, and more focus as you rekindle your relationship with the present. When you begin to pursue these activities, you will learn that your thoughts are only your feelings, your mind's inventions and that you have the power to let them move through and, then, live in the present moment with full focus.

PRINCIPLES OF MEDITATION

I've identified eight guiding principles of meditation in my practice. Each theory below is based on my experience, but I owe a lot of credits to Jon Kabat-Zinn, one of the leading mindfulness meditation teachers. They wrote extensively about meditation and helped me on my journey. Feel free to come back to this section to get grounded before you start a practice or check-in after meditation to see how these concepts influenced your practice and how they appear in your life (because they start to show up, over and over again).

Endurance

When you continue to meditate, you'll find your brain is going to work hard to get your attention: What was that sound? Did I turn it off? I wonder what it is that Joe does. This is always going to happen, and it's very natural. You may begin to find physical distractions—your leg can sleep, or you may want to fidget to make it more comfortable—as well as external distractions, such as a bird chattering or the ringing of the door. Your mind is tempted to pursue any diversion, and that might frustrate you.

Patience

Recognize the distractions, let them go (unless your leg is asleep, in which case you will adjust), and return your attention to your work. Enter each meditation with a mindset of patience, so you're prepared to accept anything that comes up, including your frustrations or doubts.

Acceptance

Acceptance goes hand in hand with patience and means that whatever you experience, whether it's an external sound or sensation or an internal thought or emotion, you accept fully. With practice, you'll start embracing everything you feel in meditation and beyond. Acceptance is meditation, in many ways.

Non-Judgmental Awareness

The idea of non-judgmental consciousness is one of the essential concepts in meditation. Our minds are deciding on almost everything. That was rude, that tastes bad, it's too cold, I'm overweight, she looks good, and so on. In an attempt to organize and understand the universe, we compare, categorize, and label: turning off this judging impulse may be challenging, but it is incredibly worthwhile. Meditation helps us to practice non-judgmental awareness and allows us to put space between our experience and our reaction so that we can actually observe what is happening. When new ideas, sounds, tastes, and feelings clamor for our attention, we are clearly aware—no marking, no judgment.

Compassion

We are born with an inherent capacity for compassion, and as we evolve, it continues to develop. We learn that if we hit or pull hair, it hurts someone else. We're finding that certain people are less fortunate. We learn to make others feel good, which makes us feel good. Meditation for compassion is powerful. It takes away our fears and our pride and emotional responses, showing that we are all human beings under the surface. As you experience this stripping away more often through meditation, you might begin to feel a liberating humility that manifests itself as a deep reservoir of compassion for yourself and others.

Forgiveness

If you're not so easily upset by incidents, situations, or even your feelings, you'll find it much easier to let go of grudges and practice acceptance as you learn to embrace all things outside of your control, without judgment and with consideration for yourself and others. Forgiveness can take you even deeper into the principles of meditation, and with several practices in this book, we will explore that concept.

Confidence

As you explore a state of being that is calming your thoughts, your mind will try all kinds of tricks to get back into the driver seat. You can feel a sudden burst of fear, or suspicion, or annoyance. Often the uplifting feelings or emotions may be strong enough, maybe even intense enough to drag you away. That's perfect. All of that is part of the operation. But, meditation is an activity worthy of your faith. If something pulls you out of it, then believe that getting back in is worthwhile. Believe in what they do for you. Trust it's there for you always. Over time this confidence will help you get more out of your practice of meditation.

Nonattachment

We tend to be valuable about our stuff, our thoughts, our ideas, and our preferences. We are getting attached to the results that we want. Nonattachment reminds you not to hold on to anything; all things are impermanent, all experiences, and all beings. This attitude helps us in our work and when we go about our daily lives.

Non-striving

For some people, this concept can be daunting, especially those who are perfectionists or overachievers. We were taught to align with our goals and approach issues to achieve or move forward. The concept of non-striving teaches us to observe clearly, without the incentive or the intention to accomplish something. The purpose of every practice of meditation is only to bring your awareness to the present moment. That is everything you have to do.

Stopping to meditate can seem crazy when there's so much else to do. Yet not having time for oneself is a big part of the dilemma that we are dealing with here, a big part of why you may feel so depressed or have trouble sleeping. If it's beneficial, instead of thinking of meditation as taking away time from other, "more important," stuff you need to do, think about meditation as the resource that helps you to be more concentrated, clearer-headed, and more effective during the rest of your day.

MBSR / MBCT

When you're still uncertain about the therapeutic effects of body and mind meditation, find these two methodologies of medical care that combine the concepts of meditation and mindfulness. The efficacy and success of these therapies show the incredible effects of meditation based on research. I urge you to do more work if one of these treatments sounds good for you or someone you love.

Mindfulness-Based Stress Reduction (MBSR)

In the 1970s, MBSR was founded by Jon Kabat-Zinn, one of the first scholars to introduce systematic empirical analysis into the field of meditation and mindfulness in order to treat a variety of problems that were difficult to handle in traditional medical settings. An eight-week course, MBSR incorporates meditation on mindfulness, the consciousness of the body, and yoga to help people reduce stress and relax. MBSR systems have been applied to hospitals globally, large companies, and even in the United States Committee. MBSR is used as complementary medicine, and most medical schools have adopted some form of MBSR education. Throughout the United States, thousands of MBSR teachers have been trained and lead programs.

Mindfulness-Based Cognitive Therapy (MBCT)

MBCT is an eight-week group therapy program founded in the early 1990s by John Teasdale, Zindel Segal, and Mark Williams' respected mindfulness research team. The software builds on the Kabat-Zinn built MBSR system. MBCT was originally created for helping people with depression by combining traditional psychotherapy approaches with mindfulness techniques. (MBSR is more general). Biochemical factors play an important role in depression, but so do the thoughts and the relationship between a person and them. Using mindfulness meditation techniques, MBCT helps patients perceive their emotions as impermanent creations ("events") of their minds, rather than real "self" representations. MBCT was found to be beneficial for depression and is now being tested for several other health applications, including diabetes and cancer.

Chapter 5: Guided Meditation To Prevent Panic Attacks And To Manage Them

People with anxiety issues are consistently exposed to constant focusing on conclusions of fear, and pessimistic thinking. For example, various people with panic issues contribute vitality and struggle with the future or stressing over the past. Fortunately, loosening up strategies can help kill these symptoms.

Loosening up techniques are practices you can adapt alone, or with the help of a specialist. These activities are anticipated to help you in upsetting your contemplations, surrendering weight, and opening up to significant loosening up. Such techniques can help balance the countless amount of mental and physical appearances of panic issue and anxiety.

What Is Mindfulness Meditation

Mindfulness thought is a releasing system that helps you to profit from your consideration to the present. During mindfulness practice, the meditator enables bits of knowledge to create without trying to stop or denounce them. For instance, dreadful examinations identified with dread, judgment, inadequacy, and stress may come up. Meditation is the demonstration of seeing these considerations and enabling them to pass.

Mindfulness meditation depends upon the probability that a huge number of individuals push away or overlook their present considerations and sentiments. Many recognize that on the off chance that they neglect negative contemplations, and then those assessments will just leave. Regardless, meditation genuinely engages you to pull back from negative sense by going toward considerations without response.

By giving awkward considerations a chance to go without responding, you can build up another reaction to dread and uneasiness. After some time, and with training, mindfulness meditation can help make internal congruity, lucidity, and harmony.

Getting Started

When you initially start to rehearse mindfulness meditation, it might be useful to do as such in a calm area that is free from distraction. The season of day you choose to contemplate can be dictated by your specific needs. For example, a few people like to begin the three-day weekend with meditation, diminishing morning nervousness and setting a reasonable and constructive tone for the afternoon. Others like to ruminate during the evening, relinquishing the worry of the day, and getting ready for a decent night's rest.

Step by step instructions to Begin Meditation

Attempt to put aside, at any rate, five to 10 minutes to sit in meditation, continuously expanding the length as you become progressively all right with your training.

- Start off sitting or resting in an agreeable position.
- Close your eyes and start your meditation with a breathing activity.
- Next, just notice your musings, enabling any plans to ring a bell.
- Keep a nonjudgmental mentality as you let yourself stay in the present with your inward voice.
- When your meditation feels total, take a couple of full breaths and open your eyes.

Mindfulness meditation may sound straightforward enough; however, even routine meditators think that it is troublesome every now and then. Truth be told, numerous individuals experience uplifted tension when they initially plunk down to think. Inspiration and want may likewise wind down from every day, so attempt to be understanding with yourself and your meditation practice.

In the event that you stick with your meditation practice, you will figure out how to sit with awkward contemplations. Just through standard practice will mindfulness meditation become less testing, help you to bring down tension, and present to you a feeling of internal harmony.

Meditation is a demonstrated way to radically diminish a fit of anxiety just as the recurrence and power of the assaults. Meditation is the demonstration of being still and making space among yourself and your issues. It has demonstrated remedial powers and can detectably lessen alarm. It disturbs over the top and negative idea examples and after that enables us to rebuild our musings.

The motivation behind Meditation for Panic Attacks

The motivation behind meditation is not to destroy challenges in a moment. Rather, the motivation behind meditation for panic attacks, tension and stress are to enable you to step away from these encounters and witness them nonjudgmentally from a separation. When we are tangled in restless considerations, battling against them, we are too caught to even think about dealing with them.

Meditation enables you to turn out to be still and calm, focused. Never again entrapped by issues, you can exist uninhibitedly. This separation enables you to just watch yourself and your circumstances. As opposed to whipping against tension and stress, which can prompt panic attacks, you have space to move around and settle on decisions with respect to your activities.

This calm, far off space carries harmony and the capacity to manage pressure and tension in a manner that does not confine your life. Acknowledgment and responsibility treatment calls this defusion since you are defusing, or isolating, from your inconveniences. Bergland (2015) considers it the ability to disregard. Whatever you call it, meditation is not tied in with disposing of issues yet is rather about helping you make the separation.

Physical and Mental Advantages of Meditation for Panic Attacks

Intervention works since it produces changes in the brain and body. Various investigations have shown that meditation

- produces alpha waves in the mind, the brainwaves related to unwinding,
- induces by and large unwinding,
- increases mindfulness,
- decreases pulse,
- lowers respiratory rate,
- reduces circulatory strain,
- increases bloodstream to the cerebrum, and
- physically changes the cerebrum and its conduct.

At first, these progressions are fleeting and practically impalpable. At the point when meditation is a standard piece of your life, the progressions become lasting and you can feel the harmony and quiet.

How to Use Mediation for Panic Attacks

Kinds of Meditation

There is definitely not an incorrect method to reflect. As you figure out how to utilize meditation for uneasiness, panic attacks, and stress, attempt these various strategies to perceive what feels directly for you.

- Structured meditation includes utilizing a center article (something in the room, an item you hold, and so on.). Inhale gradually and profoundly, and focus on your article. At the point when your mind meanders, delicately return your concentration to the article.
- In unstructured meditation, you do not attempt to focus on anything. You simply let your considerations meander without judging or adhering to any of them.
- Mantra meditation utilizes a solitary syllable, word, or expression. This sets well with insistence. Rehashing an assertion while thinking causes, you center just as rebuild your considerations.
- Breathing meditation makes them tally your breaths, either quietly or so anyone might hear. All meditation includes breathing gradually and profoundly; this sort utilizes breath-meaning fixation.
- Mindset meditation utilizes representation to help make the existence you need. Like attestations, perception enables you to hold a picture of your qualities and dreams and focus on it. This

trains your mind to move its concentration from tension to your qualities.

Meditation for Uneasiness Tips

Sitting discreetly and quieting the brain does not come effectively for people. Utilize these tips to develop an intervention for nervousness practice.

•Be quiet with yourself. Meditation for tension, panic attacks and stress is about the long run, not handy solutions.

•Drop the "shoulds" and unforgiving desires you have for yourself. A major piece of meditation is allowing contemplations to travel in many directions without making a decision about them. Abstain from making a decision about yourself and how you are ruminating.

•Sit in an agreeable position. You do not need to be with folded legs on the floor. Resting is all right, as well, however it frequently makes individuals nod off.

•Pay regard for your breath, keeping it profound and moderate. Take in through your nose and out through your mouth.

- Find a spot that is calm and when you will not be upset. Keep your telephone out of your meditation space.
- When you see on edge contemplations, stresses, and forceful feelings, simply let them be. Meditation is not tied in with banishing your considerations yet is tied in with removing yourself from them.
- Ritualize your meditation practice. Do it the same number of days every week as is sensible for you, locate a reliable time, and make your space charming.

Meditation for anxiety works. By separating yourself, quieting your cerebrum, and embracing a non-judgmental mentality, you will, after some time, radically lessen anxiety, panic attacks, and stress.

Guided Meditation for Panic Attacks Exercise

Panic attack reactions can be frightening. Overcoming panic attacks is possible with loosening up. Here is a loosening up substance for crushing panic attacks by checking out calming affirmations and encouragement. Use this guided loosening up for overseeing panic attacks at the time. Signs and indications of panic attacks incorporate physical panic attack side effects and passionate anxiety. In the event that you are encountering a panic attack now, you are presumably very frightened... what's more, that is all right in light of the fact that it is ordinary. Unwinding can assist you with defeating panic attacks and coming back to a condition of quiet. Unwinding is a typical procedure, as well.

You are not appearing, at any rate, a touch of generosity attack. You are experiencing a run of the mill, ordinary anxiety that is planned to help your body handle irritating conditions. We should begin the route toward beating panic attacks and enabling that to anxiety decay.

Pay regard to your physical position right now. You may stand, sitting, resting, or moving around. Just observe where your body is.

By and by if you have to, you can make a couple of acclimations to be progressively pleasant. You may need to plunk down, or expand a bit... or on the other hand, even rests if you like. Just empower yourself to end up being to some degree all the more physically pleasant.

Since you are in a continuously pleasant position, you can watch your condition. Is there any approaching danger? In case there is something that will cause you to hurt, you can make a transition to secure yourself. If there is no fast hazard to your life, I can promise you that right now you are shielded from harm.

The panic that you are experiencing will not hurt you. Despite the way that it may feel like you are in hazard because of this anxiety, and it is absolutely normal to feel that way... you are not in a hazard. Anxiety will not hurt you.

Anxiety attacks can be disturbing, yet they will pass. This anxiety will pass. Vanquishing panic attacks is conceivable.

You are breathing... what's more, you are getting enough air. In the event that you were not, you would not be cognizant at the present time. Your body knows how much air it needs.

On the off chance, that it feels like you cannot regain some composure at the present time, you most likely are breathing a lot of air in, however not breathing out enough. We can fix that at the present time. Victory through your lips, as though you are blowing air through a straw. Hear the air whoosh out, purging your lungs totally.

Notice how your lungs normally refill with no exertion as you naturally take in.

Breathe out again through your mouth, blowing the freshen up.

Also, breathe in.

Continue breathing naturally... making a point to breathe out totally with every breath.

You are all right at this moment. Panic attack indications are upsetting, yet they are not risky. You are not in any peril, regardless of whether you feel physical uneasiness.

You may see that anxiety is beginning to diminish. On the off chance that the anxiety has not started to diminish yet, realize that it will very soon. Anxiety cannot keep going forever. It is inconceivable for your body to keep up this state.

At some point or another, regardless of what you do, you will feel quieter. Defeating panic attacks is conceivable.

Maybe your muscles are turning into somewhat more relaxed... Perceive how you can bring down your shoulders to a nonpartisan position. They were most likely raised and tense a couple of minutes prior, however, now you can hold them lower... looser... as the muscles on the highest points of your shoulders become somewhat more and looser.

Indeed, even your jaw is presumably extricating, unwinding, enabling your mouth to be loose and free, your teeth not contacting.

Feel your breathing moving back... twisting up imperceptibly progressively moderate... deeper... your breathing is quiet... quiet and calm...

Your examinations may be all the more peaceful currently, too. In case you should reiterate a couple of affirmations to empower your thoughts to end up being fundamentally dynamically peaceful, you can go over the going with articulations after I state them. Or then again, if you like, you can essentially tune in and loosen up.

How about we start the affirmations now:

I am protected at this moment.

Defeating panic attacks is conceivable.

I am ready to manage this.

I realize that anxiety cannot hurt me.

Anxiety is a characteristic and typical procedure, and it will pass.

It is all right to be on edge.

It is all right disliked feeling on edge.

I acknowledge the manner in which I feel now, fortunate or unfortunate.

It is consummately protected to have a dashing heart...

... Also, I can feel my pulse ending up moderate and ordinary.

I realize that I am getting enough air.

My muscles are beginning to unwind.

My eyelids are feeling overwhelming.

I am beginning to feel quiet.

I am more loosened up right now than I was a minute back.

My unwinding increments as time passes.

My feelings of trepidation cannot hurt me at this moment.

My psyche can concentrate on pictures of harmony and wellbeing.

I can picture a loosening up spot at the present time.

I can envision what it might feel want to be totally loose.

I can envision what it would feel like if my hands were loose.

I can envision how overwhelming my arms would feel on the off chance that I was loose.

I can envision what unwinding feels like.

I can envision a sentiment of unwinding filling my body and psyche.

My entire body is beginning to feel loose and overwhelming.

I am protected at the present time.

I am feeling more settled.

There is nothing I need to do to feel more relaxed.

My body and psyche can loosen up all alone.

Since you have heard a few confirmations, you may see that you are much quieter than you were previously. You will likely find that you are feeling loose and even somewhat tired.

To further extend your unwinding and enable you to accomplish a condition of complete serenity, you can consider your breaths they arrive.

Without attempting to change your taking in any capacity, just notice every breath as the air goes easily all through your body.

Calmly inhale in, and as you inhale out, say "one" in your psyche. Sit tight for the following breath, and as you breathe out, tally "two."

Keep on tallying every breath for a few more couples of minutes. Continue considering I talk.

In the event that you lose tally anywhere en route, essentially start again at "one." It does not make a difference in what number of breaths you tally, or how quick or moderate your breathing is. Basically direct your concentration toward every breath, perceiving how your body inhales normally with no contribution from you. Notice and tally every breath.

(pause)

You are currently feeling profoundly loose. Completely loose and agreeable. Quiet and tranquil.

Notice how you can utilize attestations and unwinding to deal with panic attacks and decline manifestations of anxiety and panic. Defeating panic attacks is conceivable. Unwinding is compelling in conquering panic attacks. Notice how you normally come back to a condition of quiet. Retain this casual state. You can come back to this casual inclination whenever you have to.

When you are prepared to continue your normal exercises, enable your brain and body to stir, while keeping up a sentiment of quiet.

Give your muscles a chance to stir by rolling your shoulders... presently turn your head... move your arms and legs a little...

Return your regard for your environment, seeing where you are, and taking in the earth around you.

When you have come back to your typical degree of sharpness and attentiveness, you can continue your standard exercises, feeling quiet.

This one is another great exercise for panic attacks:

For this preparation, you can sit or you can stand, or you can set down. Basically get settled, with your back commonly straight, your body free and your heart open. I need you to envision that you are in your kitchen, you are at a counter, and on the counter, there is a cutting board, there is a lemon and there is a blade.

Pick up the lemon, stroll over to the sink, turn on the water and wash the lemon.

The water is cool, and feel it against your hand, turn the water off, take a paper towel, dry the lemon, truly feel the towel in your grasp, feel the lemon and after that stroll back to where the cutting board is lying on the counter.

Put the lemon down on the cutting board, keep one hand on your lemon and get the blade in your other hand.

Feel the heaviness of the blade in your grasp, it is somewhat substantial in light of the fact that it is a heavy blade, and now keeping one hand on the lemon take your blade and cut the lemon down the middle.

When you cut through that lemon, a tad of lemon, juice squirts out and you feel it on your hand and its virus.

Now you have half of the lemon in one hand, I need you to put that half down on the counter over the cutting board and I need you to slice through it once more.

A minimal more lemon juice squirts out and now you have a wedge of lemon. Put your blade down on the counter, take the wedge of lemon and I need you to put it up simply without you even noticing and take a full breath in.

Now remove a bit from that lemon—did anything occur, did your mouth water or did it pucker up?

I like such a large number of individuals your mouth watered or you puckered up simply considering that lemon then you simply had a mind-body reaction. Mindful breathing is perfect for relieving panic attacks.

You can learn cautious breathing by following the substance underneath, postponing rapidly after every entry. Go for a hard and fast time of at least a rate of five minutes.

Now take two or three minutes to compliment yourself that you are saving some exertion for meditation.

Become aware of your breath. By and by getting consideration regarding the breath the guts or midriff, breathing ordinarily and regularly.

Stay with your breath. As you inhale, think about the inhale; as you breathe back out, think about breathing out. If it is valuable, place your hands on your belly to feel it develop with each internal breath and contract with each exhalation. Essentially, what you are doing is keeping up this consideration regarding the breath, taking in and breathing out. If you cannot feel the breath in your stomach, find some other way—place your hands on your chest, or feel the improvement of air all through your noses.

Basically, be. There is no convincing motivation to envision, disregard, or comprehend the breath. Basically, you are monitoring taking in and out. Without judgment, basically watching, feeling, experiencing the breath as it forward and backward developments. There is no spot to go and nothing else to do. Essentially being in right here and now, mindful of your breathing, living one internal breath and one exhalation at some random minute.

Feel what your body is doing regularly. As you inhale, feel the abdomen or belly develop or rise like an inflatable balloon, by then feel it withdrawing, crumbling, or falling on the exhalation. Just riding the surges of the breath, step by step, inhaling in and out.

Perceive your winding character. Every so often, you may see that your thought has wandered from the breath. When you see this, basically perceive your mind wandered and perceive where it went, and after that take your thought delicately back to the breath.

Be the spot you are. Remember, there is no other spot to go, nothing else you need to do, and no one you should be right now. Essentially taking in and breathing out. Breathing ordinarily and typically, without controlling the breath in any way, just checking the breath as it returns and forward.

Perceive your time. As you arrive at the completion of this contemplation, salute yourself that you put aside this push to be accessible and that you are really growing internal resources for recovering and success. Allow us to delay for a moment to end this contemplation with the craving "May all animals discover a feeling of happiness."

Here are three basic and speedy meditation methods you can use to help get you to escape stress, away from tension and even end a fit of anxiety in its tracks.

1. Tying down

Perhaps the most ideal approaches to quiet yourself down is to grapple yourself by coordinating yourself into the lower half of your body. Start by concentrating on your feet and how they feel inside your socks or shoes and against the ground. Extend your self-regarding the incorporation of the sensations first in your lower legs and afterward, in your upper legs – do they feel substantial or light? Warm or cool? Tingly or numb? Presently incorporate the impressions of your breathing, truly unwinding as you inhale out.

This is an incredible method for mooring yourself and you can do it whenever, with your eyes open or shut, while sitting or even while strolling around. Grapple yourself. At that point, relax.

2. Breath checking

This technique can be used and identified with verifying or in solitude. Remain first. On your next in-breath, consider up to 6 you breathe in right in, and after that on the out-breath, consider up to 10 you breathe in such a separation out. This procedure has the effect of stretching both the in-breath and the out-breath, blocking your unwinding. It also broadens the out-breath more than the in-breath, compelling you to release more carbon dioxide, moving back your heartbeat, calming you down and restoring an excited equalization.

Guarantee you fit the numbers to your breath and not an alternate way. In case 6 and 10 do not work for you, find another extent that does, as long as the out-breath is in any occasion two seconds longer than the in-breath. If it is too hard to even think about the evening, think about keeping the breathing while simultaneously counting, meaning one full breath, by then taking one normal breath and count the accompanying one.

In case you feel solidified and can't manage the checking, state "in" to yourself as you take in, and "out" as you breathe out totally, endeavoring to draw out the out-breath. Then again, state "in" on the in-breath, etc. Prop up for in any occasion one minute anyway go for whatever time span that you need. I have used this strategy in all regards successfully myself to turn away approaching attacks of tension in the night.

3. Finger Breathing

Finger breathing is another rendition of counting breaths. Hold one of your hands in front of you, palm looking towards you. With the forefinger of your other hand, follow up the outside length of your thumb while you breathe in, stopping at the highest point of your thumb and afterward follow it down the opposite side while you breathe out. That is one breath. Follow up the side of the following finger while you take in, delay at the top, and afterward follow down the opposite side of that finger while you inhale out. That is two breaths. Continue onward, following along each finger as you tally every breath. When you get the finish of the last finger, return up that finger and do it in invert.

This training gives you something visual to concentrate on and something kinesthetic to do with your hands. Just by concentrating on your counting is helping you to become relaxed. It is helpful when there is a great deal circumventing you and it is hard to simply close your eyes and concentrate inwards. It is likewise an extremely simple system to show young people and children.

Chapter 6: Manifest Your Ideal Workday In Five Minutes | 5 Minutes | 342 Words

Hello and welcome to this five minute meditation for manifesting your ideal work day. Today we will explore simple questions to show you how to integrate your desired reality with everyday experiences. It is designed to be listened to before work, but you can listen to it any time you wish.

Simply close your eyes. Relax into your chair. Let everything go like flower petals in a breeze.

Bring your awareness to your breath.

Feeling the sensation as air enters your body, and leaves your body.

How your body feels as you relax into the present moment.

Letting your work go for a moment, and all of your responsibilities.

Letting your body relax.

Without any judgement, allow your answers to these questions to flow through your body. Whatever your first positive impulse is, go with that.

How did you feel today? Happy? Positive? Energized? Imagine you could feel that emotion in your body now. Allow your answers to flow through your body physically.

What did you accomplish? Feel as though you have already accomplished it now, and how wonderful it is.

How proud are you of yourself about your work day? Feel it in your body

How effortless was your day?

How full of gratitude were you about your job? Pick something that you feel grateful towards.

What did you learn today?

What did you like about your work today?

What was your favorite part of the day? You can make this up, just imagine you had a great day and pick an imaginary highlight.

What tiny goal that you have did you accomplish today?

Coming back to your breath….

Coming back into your current surroundings. Take a moment to let it all settle in. Open your eyes if they were closed.

Thank you for listening to this meditation. Feel free to listen to it as many times as you wish. It is designed to have you perceive your work in a new way, so the more times you listen to it, the stronger it gets. Have a wonderful work day today.

Five Minute Refresh | 5 Minutes | 241 Words

Hello and welcome to this five minute refresh meditation. In this meditation I will show you how to experience relaxation at any point in the day.

Bringing your awareness to your feet, allow them to tense up for ten seconds. Breathe deeply and in a relaxed way as you do this. On your exhalation relax your muscles and enjoy the sensation.

Now to your lower legs, tense it up but not to the point of pain, just gentle contraction for ten seconds, and release.

For your upper legs, contract the muscles here for ten seconds... and release.

For your pelvic floor area, groin, and buttocks, contract the muscles here for ten seconds... and release.

For your abdomen contract the muscles here for ten seconds... and release.

For your back contract the muscles here for ten seconds... and release.

For your chest contract the muscles here for ten seconds... and release.

For your upper arms contract the muscles here for ten seconds... and release.

For your lower arms contract the muscles here for ten seconds... and release.

For your hands contract the muscles here for ten seconds... and release.

For your neck contract the muscles here for ten seconds... and release.

For your face contract the muscles here for ten seconds... and release.

Take one breath in... and out.

Just let your whole body enjoy the relaxation.

Thank you for listening to this meditation today. Have a refreshing rest of your day.

Chapter 7: The White Horse

Relax and make yourself really comfortable, take a few deep breaths before we start our Guided Meditation.

Imagine you are going for a nice evening stroll in to the countryside in late summer when the evening is long and warm and the heat from the sun during the day is still in the air and on the ground. You have light and comfortable clothes and shoes on.

You walk and walk and enjoy every step of the way. One of the real joys of summer is to make more of the summer evenings and getting yourself out on foot. You feel relaxed and very comfortable.

You are walking through a meadow which is rich in wildflowers, a host of wildlife providing courtship displays and nesting. There is an abundance of pollinating insects including bees. You are surrounded by this beauty and you are feeling really good. You continue to walk until you come to a style which you have to climb over.

By now it is getting slightly darker and the sun has started to set. The sky takes on shades of orange, the colour that gives you hope that the sun will set only to rise again tomorrow.

You start to climb over the style and jump in to the next field. This field has a lot of trees in it so is looking much darker and the sun is fading only to be replaced by a stunning bright moon. You see the bright light of the moon reflecting beautifully over your skin. Just as the sun has healing energy, so does the moon. You decide to lie down and bathe in the full moons healing light. You close your eyes for a few moments, and when you open them again you see in the distance a brilliant white, the most stunning horse looking at you. He stands still and silent. You can not

Believe your eyes!This beautiful creature slowly starts to walk towards you. You stand perfectly still so as not to frighten him away. He is the most beautiful horse you have ever seen. He eventually comes walking over to you and starts to rub his head against you as if you say Hello. He is so very friendly but has an air of loneliness about him. The horse is alone and you are alone too. He bends down for you and allows you to climb on to his back, you manage to get on to this lovely horse and he very gently starts to stand up for you. You feel very safe and feel that the horse is looking after you and is here for a reason. He turns back around and walks very slowly to get you used to him. You won't fall off and anyway is he looking after you.

He continues to walk. You have no idea at all where he is taking you to. You discover that the horse is life itself, a metaphor but also an example of life's mystery and unpredictability.

This beautiful white shiny horse starts to trot and you are still feeling very safe, but before you know it, he starts to gallop. You gallop and you feel almost at one with this magical white horse that literally came out of nowhere!

He gallops faster and faster and you manage to hold on to him and you feel totally invigorated by the ride, your hair is flying all over and the moonlight is catching all the movements of the horse. He is captivating with the light on every muscle and his white mane turns to silver in this moonlight. You simply cannot take your eyes off such beauty. Your problems and anxiety have disappeared altogether.

He turns in to another field and slows down as he approaches a very deep but still lake. You can't even see a ripple from the water but you can see the moonlight reflecting on the still motionless water. The lovely horse edges closer and closer towards the lake. The moonlight seems to get bigger and bigger as you get nearer to the edge. The skies are full of stars and the moonlight on this horse is stunning.

The horse very gently bends down to allow you to jump off his back and you stand for a moment or two mesmerized by the silence and stillness of the water. The water is still warm from the hot summers day and you take your shoes off and sit down on the very edge of the lake and dip your toes in to it. The warmth immediately relaxes you and makes you feel sleepy.

You look up for a moment and notice your own reflection in the lake and the white horse is standing directly behind you. You both have a reflection in the lake. It is like a mirror it is so still.

It dawns on you at that moment that all your problems back home are so small, your anxiety has gone, depression and worries don't really exist. Your mind and brain have been tormenting you for months. Your brain produces thoughts all the time but you don't have to believe them. They are only thoughts!Not fact.

The horse seems to look at you with a knowing, he knows what your worries have been and he is trying to show you that this simple lake and moonlight which costs nothing at all and is free is the most beautiful thing you have experienced in a long time. Its magical! The horse is magical and it's a dream. You have escaped your thoughts for a while. You can escape your thoughts every time you allow yourself to go somewhere else in your mind. Nothing in your mind is ever as bad as it seems and if you can escape for a few mins you will look back and realise this. Try and create space between you and your thoughts so that you can react more calmly and allows you to catch negative thought patterns before they tip you down in a downward spiral. It begins the process of putting you back in control. You have learned something very special this evening and you feel like you are back in control. The lovely white horse bends down again for you to climb back on to his back. He gallops off at great speed with you feeling marvellous and you can't thank him enough for bringing you back down to earth again. He takes you straight back to where you found him and allows you to climb off him. You both stare at each other for a while and he turns around and trots off. You look for him in the dark but he has gone.

You turn around and go back over that style and back across the fields and take yourself off home.

You have to ask yourself was that a dream? Was it real?But it made You switch off from yourself for a while.

Remember Life is 10% what happens to you and 90% how you react to it.

Chapter 8: First Week Of Meditations

We'll be prefacing the first week of meditations by focusing on a combination of self-care and awareness meditations so that you can start your meditative journey by learning how to take care of your own physical and mental self. Always keep in mind that you are only going to be able to be an effective member of society if you yourself are well taken care of, which is why self-care is essential to any healthy lifestyle.

We'll start working on our self-care regimen by using compassion based meditations and physical well-being practices, each meditative guide is accompanied by a list of ten affirmations that you can use to reinforce your meditative focus throughout the day.

1. Loving Kindness Meditations

As we've said before, it is common that individuals find it easier to be kinder and more understanding of others than they are kind and understanding of themselves. The loving kindness meditation is meant to help individuals focus their loving energy on themselves and other people. This particular form of meditation has been linked to a decrease in chronic pain and borderline personality disorder, as well as marital conflict, anger management and social anxiety.

Start by finding a quiet corner, or a safe space where you are not likely to be disturbed. Choose a spot with a clear natural view like a park or a garden, or alternatively, just try to position yourself faced outward so that you can feel a little bit of sunlight as you begin the process. Generally upright postures are recommended for this particular exercise, such as seated or standing meditative poses. Once you feel comfortable in the position you have selected, try to clear your mind of any worries or stresses.

You are now ready to begin your meditative journey.

Breathe deeply and exhale. As you do, allow your eyes to slowly rest upon your lashes. Shed your worries and anxieties as you begin to relax your soul.

Breathe.

In the corner of your mind's eye you see a timer. Use it to slowly count down from ten, breathing in at each even number, and then slowly releasing your breath as you come across each odd number.

One.

Exhale.

Two.

Inhale.

Three.

Exhale.

Four.

Inhale.

Five.

Exhale.

Six.

Inhale.

Seven.

Exhale.

Eight.

Inhale.

Nine.

Exhale.
Ten.
Inhale.
Carefully, arch your back and as you tip your face towards the warm sunlight, allow your body to relax, and return to the present moment.

Focus your attention first on your shoulders, and begin by allowing your left shoulder to stretch up, and then backward and then down again. Enhance your relaxation by then allowing your right shoulder to do the same.

Feel the present moment engulf you.

Envision yourself in your mind's eye.

Today your task is to send kindness to yourself.

Begin by reminding yourself that you are a happy, positive person for whom positivity is a way of life.

As you do, remind yourself of the following -

There is nothing that you cannot do, you are a capable and confident individual.

There is nothing you are afraid of; fear and negativity cannot touch you because to you, failure is but another step in the right direction.

The present moment allows you to live in a happy, fulfilled manner – so much so that you are forever free of pain and unhappiness.

You are free of pain.

You are free of negativity.

You are free of difficulty.

Visualize yourself in your mind's eye. Identify your flaws, and as you do direct a ray of love directly to the flaws that your perceive.

Know that you are more than the flaws you fear.

You are strong.

You are capable.

You are loved, and you are worth loving.

Bend your neck forward and back, counting to five, as you do.

Release the stress you can feel building in your body, and as you do you will feel your body grow lighter with the love and kindness that floods through it in a wave or iridescent light.

Breathe in and release.

You are whole, and loved.

You are vital. Your vitality is such that you are invaluable to yourself and to your surroundings.

The universe needs you.

Your family and friends love and need you.

Breathe in again and release.

Today in this moment you choose to live life with ease and happiness, your happiness being so powerful that it frees you from all forms of pain.

Breathe out. You are now a loved and compassionate individual.

Bonus Affirmations

Today my heart is filled with kindness and love, and nothing else exists.

Every breath that I take into my body is filling me with love and happiness, and every breath that I expel is purging negativity from my soul.

Today I am the manifestation of love. I am in love with myself and the goodness of others. My love vibrates around me like a protective casing protecting me from harm and danger.

I am like a magnet that attracts kindness, compassion and all things good and right.

I am a worthy vessel who is filled with infinite and unending positivity and compassion.

I am respectful of my body. My body has loved and housed my soul with gentleness and compassion and I hope to be as kind and generous to it as possible.

I am honored to be the person I am. My perception of myself is positive and kind.

I am filled with a great ability to love and today I choose to direct that love unto myself.

I am forgiving of myself and the mistakes that I make because I know and understand that to err is human and my ability to love myself supersedes such mistakes.

My life is a gift and I choose to look upon it with confidence and compassion.

2. Mantra Meditation

Mantra meditation is meant to teach the participant how to best match their intention to their meditation, which in turn helps attune them with the wavelength they wish to be on. The term mantra refers to a syllable, a word or a phrase that the practitioner wants to imbed in their subconscious in a way that will preface all conscious and subconscious thoughts and actions. Usually Sanskrit terms such as 'Om' and 'Jai' are used to build a sort of focus based 'dhyan' or meditative lull. This allows you to transform your consciousness.

Once again, find yourself a quiet corner, or a safe space where you are not likely to be disturbed. Mantra meditations can be done in both prostrate and upright positions, although upright postures are recommended, like sitting or standing.

Once you feel comfortable in the position you have selected try to clear your mind and steady your breathing.

You are now ready to begin your meditative journey.

Breathe in deeply three times, and as you do, begin to consciously track your air flow.

Air is flowing generously in and out of your body.

Slowly breathe in and out.
Breathe in, and out again.
In this moment, time is infinite.
You have no worries.
You have no restrictions.
Breathe in.
Release.
And relax.

Your sole focus in life at this moment is to understand the mantra that you have chosen for the day.

Slowly begin to breathe deeper and tell yourself – Every day in every way, I am growing and becoming a better and better person.

As you breathe in, count to four. As your breath travels through your system, hold still for an additional four seconds.

Release your breath steadily and as you do, consciously count to four.

Every day, you are better and better.
You are better and better in every way.
Breathe in and out.

Remind yourself that the difficulties and the obstacles that you face are simply a regular part of life, and no amount of

restraint or perfection can allow you to completely side step them.
Breathe in.
Release.
And relax.
Now, remind yourself as you relax of the times that you overcame obstacles that you were faced with. How long it took, or how difficult it was, doesn't matter.
Breathe in.
Release.
And relax.
You are better and better every day.
Your constant efforts and your persistence are what have made your life better. And your life today is better, in every way.
Breathe in.
Release.
And relax.
Today, you are surrounded by light and laughter.
Your laughter is limitless.
You are limitless.
Breathe in.
Release.
And relax.

Your joy is limitless.
You are limitless.
Breathe in.
Release.
And relax.
Your light is limitless.
You are limitless.
Breathe in.
Release.
And relax.
Today you are your own master. There is nothing you cannot do, and nothing that you cannot surpass. You are in constant and continuous growth.
Breathe in.
Release.
And relax.
For one last time, remind yourself -that every day in every way, you are growing and becoming a better and better person.
Breathe out.
Bonus Affirmations
I choose to consciously love, believe in and support my own life force.

Today I am better than I have been before, and tomorrow I will be better than I am today in this moment.

I am strong, I am courageous. I am enough.

I am a warrior. There is nothing I cannot accomplish if I set my mind to it.

I am a magnet for positivity. My ability to attract positive things allows me to give more to the people around me and that in turn allows me to grow as an individual.

In this moment, I choose to feed my spirit and soul. My body is a tool that I choose to hone, while my mind is a realm of infinite possibilities.

I can accomplish anything I set my mind to and today I endeavor to be the very best that I can be.

I am happy and healthy. My mind and body are ready to face the world and any obstacles that I am facing.

I am a person who is strongly loved and cherished. My soul is filled with bright loving energy.

I am a perfect balance of peace and energy. The universe speaks to me through my mind and my body, and I accept the gentle pace it has set for me unconditionally without fear or anxiety.

3. Body Scan Meditation

The next form of meditation that you will be learning is the body-scan. The body-scan is a form of healing meditation that is used to help individuals heal their body through deep wave meditation techniques. The pain cortex of the brain is triggered by a combination of physical and mental cues, which is why if we can carefully built the mental cues for the pain cortex to be pain free while directing healing and positive thoughts toward the flawed or disturbed area, it is possible to alleviate pain in the body. This particular meditative technique usually uses visualization techniques to practice happier and healthier thoughts in the mind.

Start by finding yourself a quiet corner, or a safe space. You need to ensure that you pick a spot where you are not likely to be disturbed for the next ten to thirty minutes. Generally, the body scan meditation is best done lying down or seated in a comfortable chair. Once you have chosen a specific meditation posture and you feel comfortable in the position you have selected, proceed to try to clear your mind and prepare for the meditative guide.

You are now ready to begin your meditative journey.

Breathe in deeply and release.

Repeat the following exercise three additional times.

Breathe in.

Hold.

And relax.

Once again –

Breathe in.

Hold.

And relax.

And finally, breathe in.

Hold.

And relax.

As you breathe in deeper and deeper, you are allowing your mind to enter a state of complete relaxation.

There is nothing and nobody else around you.

You and only you exist.

As you continue to practice your breathing, you will start to notice that a bright light has begun to shine in the upper right-hand corner of your eyes.

Breathe in.

Hold.

And relax.

Gently guide your consciousness toward the light.

Breathe deeply, and focus on your breathing.

As you come closer to the light, you will start to realize that there is a hard-wooden door just beyond the light. Open it and step in.

As you do you will see in front of you is a mirror, and as you look carefully at the mirror you will notice that certain areas on your body are lit up with a bright red light.

The bright red light is showing you the areas on your body that are in need of healing.

As you have gone through life, for whatever reason, these particular areas have had to deal will some form of physical trauma which causes pain to radiate through your body.
Breathe in.
Hold.
And relax.
Today, you are going to be taking on that pain and actively healing it, so that when you awaken you are left pain free, and feeling better and better.
Breathe in.
Hold.
And relax.
Start by selecting one of the marked areas in the reflection and on your own body, mentally press your hand just above the radiating red light. Hold down and focus.
Breathe in.
Hold.
And relax.
In your mind's eye, envision every positive thought and every positive unit of energy surrounding you and travelling to that area

of pain. Slowly, you can start to feel the pain start to ebb.

Breathe in.

Hold.

And relax.

As you do you will notice that the bright red is slowly beginning to lose its brightness, and is now beginning to dull under your palm as if it is being stripped of its intensity by the powerful positive waves that you have been directing toward it.

With each bit of positive energy, you can feel your body start to heal.

Breathe in.

Hold.

And relax.

As the pain starts to subside, focus your positive energy on the next pain center, and repeat the process yet again.

Breathe in.

Hold.

And relax.

Step by step you will proceed to heal each pain centre in your body.

Breathe in.

Hold.

And relax.

You are not scared and you are not hurt.

Pain cannot touch you.

You are whole and unaffected.

Breathe in.

Hold.

And relax.

Once you have finished healing each individual area, step back out of the door and slowly come back to the present moment.

You will return to the present moment at the count of five.

One.

Two.

Three.

Four.

Five.

Awaken.

You are healthy and whole, without any form of pain impacting your physical being.

Bonus Affirmations

In this moment, I am healed, healthy and whole. My health is a part of the universe and the universe is healing me.

All of my ailments are being released into the universe and as I release my symptoms I am simultaneously drawing in soft healing light to fill my soul.

I am focusing my life-force on healing my body from the inside out. Every individual cell in my body is currently on a journey to fill my body with wellness and health.

My vitality shines from my being, and I am grateful for the good health and good fortune that has been bestowed upon me.

I am healthy and I openly embrace a healthy lifestyle. My body itself is strong and capable and I fortify this strength by feeding it healthy and nutritious food.

I am in love with all of my body's abilities, and my consciousness is actively appreciating my abilities by maintaining perfect health.

I love myself. My love for myself allows my cells to replenish my body with nourishment and energy so that my body can heal quickly and easily.

I am the only person who has control over my health, I choose to be a healthier and happier person and this choice will allow me to be happier and healthier.

My body is healthier every single day and every single day it is consciously healing itself.

My entire being is surrounded by healing energy and this energy allows me to be healthier and happier as I deserve to be.

4. Walking Meditation

The next form of meditation that we will be looking at is "walking meditation." Unlike most forms of meditation which require you to stay in a specific position, either seated, standing or prostate, walking meditation requires you to engage in walking as you continue to meditate. This particular form of meditation is intended to allow you to savour the universal practice of calm connectedness with the universe.

In order to begin, select for yourself a calm and quiet place such as a park where you can walk comfortably back and forth. While walking meditations in theory can be conducted indoors, it is strongly recommended that you try to find an appropriate outdoor location to practice this particular meditation, as this would allow you to open your senses and feel your surroundings more completely. Once you have found yourself in an appropriate place, begin by drawing in a deep breath and centering your focus on your physical self.

You are now ready to begin your walking meditation.

Start by drawing a deep breath the carefully draw in the surrounding air as you allow your eyes to carefully look around you and take in your surroundings.

Exhale carefully to the count of four.

Relax.

There is constant noise surrounding you, leaves rustling, car horns blaring, and yet at the same time with each breath the surrounding noise seems to fade away.

Breathe in.

Hold.

Exhale.

And relax.

Breathe in deeply, and as you do carefully roll your shoulders backward and forward, allowing them to ease into the lull of consciousness you are now within.

Breathe in.

Hold.

Exhale.

And relax.

As you begin to walk down the road or pathway today, you will be consciously thinking of each action that you are causing your body to undertake. You will consciously assess when you are lifting a foot, when you are moving it forward, where you are allocating pressure and how you are shifting your weight to move forward.

Breathe in.

Hold.

Exhale.

And relax.

Today you are focusing your mind and body on your inner self. Your inner self is your consciousness, and your consciousness is the puppet master that is

telling you to take each step and to lift each foot as you move forward.
Breathe in.
Hold.
Exhale.
And relax.
Today you are slowing down this consciousness so that you can keep pace, and more importantly so that you can focus your awareness on the small insignificant tasks you take part in on a daily basis.
Breathe in.
Hold.
Exhale.
And relax.
You have infinite time and infinite opportunities.
There is no rush.
You do not need to speed up or to keep up with anyone but yourself.
Breathe in.
Hold.
Exhale.
And relax.

Consciously watch as your foot moves and takes you incrementally forward with each new step.
Breathe in.
Hold.
Exhale.
And relax.
Every step you take today is a deliberate choice that you are making – this choice is what allows you to move forward.
Breathe in.
Hold.
Exhale.
And relax.
You are calm and mindful.
There is no panic or stress invading your mind.
Breathe in.
Hold.
Exhale.
And relax.
Walking comes easily to you.
Breathe in.
Hold.
Exhale.
And relax.

Once you have arrived at your destination slowly close your eyes, breathe in and open them once again.

You are whole and complete, with every step in your life.

Bonus Affirmations

Every day I am moving forward in life with strong constant steps. Each of these steps allow me to move with assurance and poise. I am strong and powerful.

Every step that I am taking I am taking consciously so that I can clean and clear my physical space. I consciously remove obstacles from my life, and my life becomes easier and happier.

As I am walking in a continuous motion, I am consciously drawing in deep, clear breaths. I breathe in happiness and joy and with each additional breath I am bringing positivity closer to my soul.

I can feel the earth under my feet as I walk. Each step brings me in contact with the energy of the earth. The earth's energy strengthens and supports my everyday life.

I am one with nature. The plants and animals that surround me are tuned in to the same wavelength in the universe, they are breathing with me in unity and we exist joyfully in unity.

My body moves freely and of its own accord as I move forward with each step.

As I breathe in I am inhaling oxygen provided to me by nature and the world, while as I breathe out I am providing nourishment to the plants and fauna that I coexist with.

Every step I take is centered with the universe, the universe is in sync with my needs and my intentions and is seeking the same things that I am.

I give to the world and to nature, and in turn nature gives back to me, air to air and life to life.

My vision of life is embodied on this path that I am walking. Each step I take forward is a step as I move closer to the goals that I have set for myself.

5. Open Awareness Meditation

The open awareness meditation is meant to allow your brain to diverge from single-minded focus and instead simply allow yourself to mesh with the universal center that we all seek. Unlike guided meditations which intend to direct your mind to a specific thought pattern, open awareness meditations are meant to allow your mind to experience the emotions that you are currently feeling. The objective here is to teach yourself that there is no reason to avoid even difficult emotions such as pain or fear. Buddhist teachings tell us that pain itself is unavoidable, while the choice to suffer is optional. Awareness meditations are meant to help you teach your mind to deal with these complex emotions without indulging in them so much so that you become a "sufferer" instead of someone who simply experiences a particular emotion.

To begin your open awareness meditation find yourself a calm safe place where you will not be disrupted for the foreseeable future. Open awareness meditation can be conducted either in an outdoor setting or in a room. Either way, the meditation is best conducted in a seated position. Look around yourself, and as you do, draw in a deep breath, and close your eyes in preparation for your meditative journey.

You are now ready to begin your open awareness meditation.

As you close your eyes, regulate your breathing to bring you more into this moment and toward a journey that allows you to open your mind to the realm of constant awareness. Keep in mind that the objective of open awareness meditation is to allow you to let down the walls of your mind in such a manner that your natural senses can start to absorb and create an awareness about themselves. In this current moment, you will notice that you are breathing in a particular way.

Carefully try to identify the nature of your every breath.

Are you currently taking short frequent breaths?

Or are you taking long deep breaths that fill your diaphragm and leave you feeling slightly fuller.

Breathe in.

Focus.
Release.
You will find that you are surrounded by distractions. At any given moment, there are hundreds of different thoughts coming to your mind, reminding you of things that you need to do, moments from the past and glimpses into the future.
Breathe in.
Focus.
Release.
Generally feelings such as this can tend to cause panic or anxiety in your life. Tasks that you failed can cause anxiety because sense that you have lost time and you no longer have the time to do it.
Breathe in.
Focus.
Release.
Incidents from your past can cause feelings of shame such make you feel that there is negativity in your life that you cannot get rid of.
Breathe in.
Focus.
Release.

Projections about the future can cause you to feel anxious and stressed because you do not know whether or not you will be able to get to where you want to be.
Breathe in.
Focus.
Release.
Keep in mind however that each of these thoughts are designed simply to move you along on the path of awareness.
Breathe in.
Focus.
Release.
Remember that every emotion comes with its own time limit. As long as you can envision the negative emotion as a separate entity from yourself, and consciously refrain from drawing it into your life source, there is no reason for the specific emotion to outlive its lifespan.
Breathe in.
Focus.
Release.
You are whole and complete.
Bonus Affirmations

I am strong, alert and attentive to the world around me. I am alert in every moment of my existence.

I am mindful of my surroundings, the present moment is what encapsulates my day, and as such I am consciously building an openness to the presence of the present.

I am focused and alive. My focus on the present is what allows me to function in a fully conscious manner, with happiness and joy lighting my way.

I am consciously seeking to experience life to the fullest by ensuring that I am paying careful attention to every moment that I exist in.

I am focusing my conscious thought pattern on the present. This clear focus is what allows me to fully appreciate all the wonderful experiences I am blessed with.

I am consciously choosing to live in a state of constant awareness of my surroundings. I am opening my senses to the world and the world fills them as it sees fit.

I am striving to be conscious and aware. My consciousness is what allows me to change the ordinary to extraordinary.

My awareness is awake and centered. By consciously choosing to be aware I am surpassing my own expectations and becoming more open everyday.

My life becomes more enriched the more aware I am of the magical surroundings that I am within.

I am consciously choosing to slow down today. My choice is what will allow me to fully appreciate my surroundings and my gifts.

6. No Religion Meditation

A major concern for many meditation minded individuals face is that they feel that they are indulging in another religion. However, it's important to remind ourselves that meditation and religion are two separate things. Despite the fact that certain religions require meditation to attain specific levels of consciousness, medication itself does not need to be religiously motivated. It is entirely possible to meditate without any religious influence or affiliation, which is why many American schools have now begun to introduce meditation as part of the school curriculum to help teach students how to control their thoughts and emotions.

Meditation that is specifically directed to avoid any form of religious connectivity is best conducted outdoors so that an individual has the opportunity to connect with the earth and the universe. This creates a basis for focusing that is not specific to any higher power that individual may or may not believe in. This form of meditative practice can be conducted in any given posture, however the recommended posture is seated, kneeling or upright.

Once you have comfortably seated yourself draw in a deep breath and release. You are now ready to begin your meditative guide. Slowly breathe in and out.

In this moment you are about to embark on a spiritual journey that allows you to travel deep into your subconscious and conscious mind, and to bring yourself into a state of complete relaxation.

Breathe.

Relax.

Hold.

And release.

Look around you and as you do carefully focus your attention on each separate breath. Remind yourself as you breathe that you are taking in oxygen from nature. Hold it deep inside your soul to actively feel the universe connect with your core, and then slowly release each breath.

Remember that you are whole and complete.

As you continue to focus on your breathing, remind yourself why you are meditating.

Breathe.

Relax.

Hold.

And release.

You are a brave, hard-working individual. You have the ability to complete tasks immaculately without making any mistakes. Perfection is part of your trade.

Breathe.
Relax.
Hold.
And release.
You are a strong courageous individual. You do not cower in the face of fear.
Breathe.
Relax.
Hold.
And release.
You are important in your community. You are needed and loved by the people around you.
Breathe.
Relax.
Hold.
And release.
Happiness and prosperity come naturally to you.
Breathe.
Relax.
Hold.
And release.
You are a happy and prosperous person.
Breathe.
Relax.

Hold.

And release.

In this moment you are seeing yourself in your mind's eye as a happy and prosperous person.

Breathe.

Relax.

Hold.

And release.

You have the ability to be all you wish to be.

No obstacle can hold you back.

You are full, and free and one with the universe.

Breathe.

Relax.

Hold.

And release.

Bonus Affirmations

I am a creature of the universe. My religion is love and my heart is my temple.

My consciousness has no religion. I am not seeking belief or ideology, I am not bound by gender or sexual orientation, I am not judged by my race or my age. I am simply the embodiment of my consciousness.

I am a vibrational being. By entire body is impacted by a web of energy that is derived from my presence and intentions.

I am my thoughts, and my thoughts are what arise from my conscious decision to be more than who I am in this moment.

I do not seek to be judged by a religion. I seek simply to be. My choices are not meant to be judged they are meant to be understood.

Religion does not dictate my morals. My morals are determined from the basic principles of right and wrong and it is upon this understanding that I open my mind.

I seek to build bridges of empathy instead of erecting walls of religion to discriminate.

I am cocooned in the loving energy of the universe, here I am safe and loved without reproach.

My life is filled with challenges that I have the ability to overcome.

In this moment, I choose to relax and cast aside all mental burdens and to allow into my very being the love the universe seeks to flood through me.

7. Zazen Breath Awareness Meditation

The last form of meditation that we will be dealing with in this first week of practice is commonly known as Zazen Meditation. This form of meditation is generally considered to be part of the Zen practices. Zen is a particular school of meditation that is part of Buddhist beliefs. Zazen itself is the study of one's own self. This particular practice is intended to teach the participant to visualize one's body, breath and mind as a cohesive unit. The Zazen meditation is best conducted in the full lotus position, Or if the particularly vicious to them, the Burmese seated position. As you seat yourself in a comfortable position, draw in a deep breath and clear your mind in preparation for the next fifteen minutes.

You are now ready to begin your meditative journey.

Allow your eyes to slowly close, as you draw breath into your body.

Breathe in to the count of four.

And hold.

One.

Two.
Three.
Four.
And release, slowly to the count of four.
One.
Two.
Three.
Four.
As you breathe, you will begin to feel energy flow through your entire body.
Your body is a vessel.
It holds within it energy and experiences that not only change your mind but also shape your perception.
Breathe in Slowly.
Hold.
And release.
One.
Two.
Three.
Four.
There is nothing in your life you are not capable of achieving.
Allow this knowledge to flow through your entire being like the air you have been drawing into your lungs.

Breathe in slowly.
One.
Two.
Three.
Four.
Hold.
And release.
One.
Two.
Three.
Four.
You are strong and in control.
Your ability to control your mind is what allows you to continuously bring it back to your central point of focus.
Breathe in slowly.
One.
Two.
Three.
Four.
Hold.
And release.
One.
Two.
Three.
Four.

As you continue to breathe in at a regular pace, you start to notice that your ability to see and perceive that your surroundings have shifted.
Your senses are now honed.
Breathe in slowly.
Hold.
And release.
One.
Two.
Three.
Four.
As your mind slowly empties itself of thought and internal conflict, it also opens itself up to new and previously unseen frontiers.
Breathe in carefully.
And count -
One.
Two.
Three.
Four.
Hold.
And release.
One.
Two.

Three.
Four.
Everything that surrounds you now has new meaning.
You can now see things that you had never noticed, and understand things you never bothered to hear.
Breathe in slowly.
One.
Two.
Three.
Four.
Hold.
And release.
One.
Two.
Three.
Four.
Allow your awareness to grow around you.
Allow your mind to meld itself in with your breathing and you physical self.
You are one and the same.
You are united with your actions.
You are complete in your thoughts.
Breathe in slowly.
One.

Two.
Three.
Four.
Hold.
And release.
One.
Two.
Three.
Four.

Bonus Affirmations

What I feel like in a fleeting moment is a visitor in my subconscious. I will allow each emotion to come and go without trapping it.

We are born again every morning and every morning we have an opportunity to do better than the day before.

I am a remarkable person. My life's joy is to find the wonder in my own being. I am a seeker of beauty and joy and every day I find both.

I am loving and loved. My ability to be gracious and giving is not limited by anything. I make no assumptions and have no expectations.

There is nothing lacking in my life, I have all that I need and as I have all that I need I have in my possession the entirety of the universe.

I am loved and loving. My lovingness is what allows me to be a light on the path for the people I love and care about.

I choose to consciously allow myself to sit back and relax. By resting my mind I am telling myself that I am enough and that I have enough.

I move to consciously visualize my life and my life is running along that positive visualization.

I choose to open my arms to constant change. As I do so I am grounding myself in the positive nature of my morals and allowing that positivity to expand.

I am gaining positivity with every step that I take and I am breaking the chains of negativity with every breath.

Chapter 10: Deepening

In order for us to dive deeper into your subconscious, I will need you to relax as much as you can. In the following few minutes, we are going to try a muscle relaxation exercise. As I mention an area, I invite you to focus on the area, so you can tense and relax it. When I tell you to tense an area, this should not cause you any pain whatsoever. If at any point you feel discomfort, please stop or try to ease up on tensing the area.

When you are ready, take a deep breath. Inhale…exhale…and we will begin.

We are first going to start with your neck and your shoulders.

To start, please try to raise your shoulders up toward your ears. As you do this, you will feel the muscles in your neck and shoulders begin to tighten. Feel the tension, where it builds, and then release. Allow your shoulders to drop to their normal position. Your shoulders and neck should feel comfortable. If not, try this again until you feel the muscles release and relax.

Remember to breathe through this process. Inhale...and exhale. Good.

Now, we will move onto your hands.

I want you to squeeze both hands into fists. Your hands are in very tight balls. You can try to pretend that you are squeezing a rubber ball. Hold this ball in your hands and feel as the tension begins to build first in your hands, and gently moves up your forearms.

When you feel the pressure, release your hands. Gently shake them and get rid of any tension. How do your hands feel now? They should feel much more relaxed.

With your neck and hands relaxed, let us draw your attention to your forehead. Our faces do a lot of activity for us through the day. Our facial expressions allow us to tell people when we are happy, sad, or stressed. I want you to raise your eyebrows. Feel as the muscles in your forehead begin to tighten and hold that position. Now, try to lower your eyebrows and tighten your eyes. Hold this tight for a few moments and then release.

Notice now how relaxed and smooth your forehead feels now that you have released the tension. Your eyelids are gently resting over your eyes, and you feel comfortable again. When you are ready, inhale…exhale…now move your focus to your jaw.

If you can, tightly close your mouth. Feel how tight your jaw feels as you clamp it closed. Your lips are tense across your teeth, and the tension builds in your jaw. Take a moment to note how this feels, and then relax your jaw. Allow your mouth to fall relaxed and loose. Release all tension and feel how wonderful and light your head feels.

To complete your relaxation, we will now practice deep breathing. Deep breathing is an excellent practice as it can help cure any stress or anxiety you may be feeling at any given moment. As you breathe, you remind your body that this is a fundament to your survival. Any time we are stressed, you may not notice, but our breathing patterns change. By doing this, it is your body's attempt to survive physical activity.

While helpful in actual dangerous situations, it won't help you if you are anxious over something that is isn't dangerous to you immediately. When our breathing becomes rapid, it also becomes shallow. Short, shallow breaths may make you feel like you are unable to catch your breath. This is because you are not breathing properly.

When we do not breathe properly, your lungs fill with stale, old air. This is not helpful as new air is unable to enter. In this sense, you need oxygen to fill yourself with positive energy. Proper breathing techniques will help you in multiple ways from relaxing to letting go of stress. When you learn to breathe the right way, you can stop the negative cycle and gain the ability to calm your body under stressful circumstances.

If you find yourself breathing too quickly, it could cause tingling, numbness, or even lightheadedness. The cure here is to learn how to slow down your breathing. Bring your focus on keeping your breath deep and full.

Now, I am going to go through a breathing exercise with you. Before we begin, I want you to take careful note of how you are breathing right now. Are your lungs full? Do you feel like you have old air stuck in there? Are your breaths quick or long?

When you are ready, I want you to inhale slowly and count to four...We will pause and count to three...and then exhale to the count of five. Ready?

Inhale...and two...and three...and four...and pause...two...three...and exhale...two...three...four...five...

Wonderful. Let us try it a few more times. Truly try to focus on each step of your breath. Trust the natural rhythm of your breathing to help relieve any anxiety or stress you may be holding onto.

Inhale...and two...and three...and four...and pause...two...three...and exhale...two...three...four...five...

Inhale...and two...and three...and four...and pause...two...three...and exhale...two...three...four...five...

Inhale...and two...and three...and four...and pause...two...three...and exhale...two...three...four...five...

Inhale...and two...and three...and four...and pause...two...three...and exhale...two...three...four...five...

Inhale...and two...and three...and four...and pause...two...three...and exhale...two...three...four...five...

With your breath in mind, it is now time to give in completely to relaxation. It is time to assure your body and mind are both set for the session. Now, I want you to repeat after me, and then we will begin.

I am gently going into a state of total relaxation

(Pause)

At this moment, my body and mind are both relaxing.

(Pause)

I am going deeper and deeper. I am relaxing deeper and deeper.

(Pause)

Every muscle in my body is relaxing. I feel peaceful. Everything around me is quiet.

(Pause)

Wonderful. Now, I am going to count from the number one to the number ten. When I reach ten, your whole body will be relaxed. You will be safe and completely calm in your mind and in your soul. When you are ready, take a deep breath, exhale, and we will begin.

One...feel as all of the muscles in your face begin to relax. You are releasing the tension from your forehead. The muscles around your eyes soften. You allow your jaw to go slack. Your face was active all day long. At this moment, it is time to give your face a rest.

Two...the muscles in your neck begin to melt. They are loosening and relaxing. Your neck worked all day to keep your head on straight. Feel as the muscles relax and melt into your pillow and bed. They can finally rest up for another day.

Three...Feel as your shoulders relax further into the bed. If there is any tension in them, shake them out gently and allow them to fall away from your ears. Many of us hold our shoulders scrunched up through the day. We do it subconsciously when we are scared, stressed, or even just cold. Allow your shoulders to relax completely and feel them fall peacefully onto the bed without a care in the world.

Four...Gently bring your focus to your hands. They are finally done for the day. They held your food for you, typed away on the computer, and held your loved one. Now, they are free of any responsibility. Give them a quick flex and relax your hands. Allow your fingers to fall away from your fists and allow them to rest wherever they are at this moment.

Five...as the rest of your body begins to rest, feel as your chest muscles relax. They follow suit from your neck and your shoulders. Focus on the lungs inside of your chest. Breathing is coming easily and naturally. Each time you breathe, you feel yourself relax further into your meditation. Peacefully, thank your lungs for doing such a wonderful job to support you.

Six...imagine the muscles in your back begin to loosen. As you lay in bed, they are finally able to relax. They worked hard all day to keep you upright and supported you when you needed them most. Now, they can relax and enjoy a good night's rest. Feel as the muscles in your back and lower back let go of any final tension.

Seven...now, the muscles in your stomach are relaxing. If you were stressed today, you might have felt a lot of tension in your stomach. This is why we use the expressions "butterflies in my stomach" or "I felt sick to my stomach." There are many connections between our psyche and our stomachs. At this moment, you have no worries. Your stomach can relax and rest for the night.

Eight...feel the muscles of your buttock begin to relax. This is a location many of us don't spend a lot of time thinking about. Feel as the muscles loosen and relax. Your buttock sinks deeper into the bed, and you feel yourself becoming even more comfortable as your body gets ready for a full night's rest.

Nine...the top of your thighs is relaxing. Your legs do so much work through the day. They allow you to walk from place to place and support you. Gently release any tension that may be built up in your legs and picture them sinking deeper and more comfortable into the bed.

Ten...finally, feel like the muscles in your lower legs relax. Your feet let go of all tension, and you find yourself completely comfortable. There is not a single place in your body holding onto tension. You feel comfortable, safe, and at peace.

Now, you are in a state of total and deep relaxation. From the top of your head to the tip of your toes, you are totally relaxed.

You are feeling better and better. You are ready to focus on sleep at the count of three.

One...

Two...

Three...

Chapter 11: Illustration Of Meditation Points

For centuries now, monks and Buddhists have achieved so much significant peace of mind. We always wonder how they have achieved it and make it part of their daily routine. The truth is it takes a lot of work, and more importantly, they had to begin from scratch. Just like all other pro mediators, a beginner needs to work hard and climb their way through to be successful. Dedication and consistency will ensure that you graduate from one state to the next until you realize your desired goal. The inner urge and notion of your progress should be left behind for better results. The key focus should be on the critical part of the journey and not the goal. This should not mean that you set goals then forget about everything. It, however, suggests that being goal-oriented may be beneficial for a project but can be a massive obstacle during meditation. When you set a goal that you intend to achieve, you may be here, but the goal is somewhere else. However, the main objective of meditation is to make both your brain and mind to be at present. Even when the mind wanders, you will find a way to allow it to come back. Also, it is impossible to escape your mind and move somewhere else. Situations like sitting can help you to rest the present moment, thus not being able to go anywhere.

Stress can cause anxiety and depression. This can also make the victims prone to heart attack and stroke. Studies have shown that people who practice meditation are less likely to die of getting a heart attack and stroke. This is because meditation dramatically reduces anxiety. How does meditation reduce anxiety? Meditation has a physiological effect in mind. During meditation, there is a significant change in brain activity. This change will lower the following: heart rate, breathing rate, adrenaline level, oxygen consumption, level of cortical, and blood pressure. Different meditation types can have physiological benefits for the body.

For instance, guided meditation uses mental images to facilitate relaxation and calmness. Transcendental meditation, on the other hand, usually uses repeated phrase or sound to help o0ne empty their mind. Lastly, mindfulness meditation focuses on the current moment and assists you in accepting situations without judgment. As you start meditation for anxiety, realize that you should start with fewer minutes, and increase as time goes by. It is straightforward to get started, and you should start with as little as one minute per day and increase your timing gradually to 10m minutes per day or even more.

As you start breathing exercises, extend the extent to which you exhale. Make it long, deep, and calmer than usual. After this, now focus on how you exhale, also make it longer than you always do. After these two exercises, breath then holds the breadth at the top when you inhale again. This can be done for 3-5 seconds or longer, depending on how one can as you continue to hold concentrate on and feel your heartbeat through your chest. You will notice that as you hold your breath longer, so does your pulse become louder. Now it is time to use simple meditation techniques. Still holding breath while at the top of inhaling, feel and listen to the sensation coming from your physical heartbeat. You can tell us the palm of your fingerprints by placing it over your heart. Find a pulse on your throat or wrist using your fingertips and feel your pulse. Pulse can also be felt in the neck, face, or near your chest.

Though keep in mind that you need to listen to the heartbeat physically. After having regular contact with the heartbeat, stop holding once you inhale. Your heartbeat or pulse will now be able to measure the length of your inhale and exhale, which should be the same. This process can be referred to as Basic Heart Rhythm Meditation. While practicing all these, you will enjoy synchronicity of breath and heart. During heart rhythm meditation, the pulse is called the echo of the heartbeat. This is because the heartbeat is felt like a double bit while the pulse is a single bit. Another way to connect and create contact with one's file is though holding palms out facing upwards.

You can take left fingers; wrap tightly under the right wrist; do this until you feel the pulse point. You can now bring your hands to the chest together. This makes you have better contact with your pulse and feel like cradling one's heart. This offers a high point of contact with the pulse while comforting your heart. These techniques help one practice on how to meditate. It is essential to know and understand that managing anxiety using healthy ways con improve one's quality of life and remove stress from the heart. Whenever something dreadful overcomes you, you feel pain in your chest, your heart begins to flutter, and you find it hard to catch your breath. These are some of the classic symptoms of anxiety, which are usually mistaken to be a heart attack. The stress hormones are released due to triggers from emotional turmoil. These, in turn, interfere with brain areas responsible for regulating cardiovascular functions like blood pressure and heart rate.

Therefore, in most cases, anxiety goes together with depression and stress. The scientist has believed that depression and anxiety are some of the expressions of shared essential biology. This is because most people who suffer from anxiety will have depression at one point in their lives. The reverse is true because most people who have depression experience some element of anxiety disorder. Long term stress that is not managed can lead to any of the two or both the conditions. There has also been a significant link between anxiety and heart disease. For example, people with high anxiety levels often have a higher risk of heart attack and other cardiac-related problems. The problem, however, is more pronounced in people with a history of heart problems. As the frequency and intensity increases, so does the risk.

Different anxiety attack has a different effect on the cardiovascular system. Many theories have been invented to explain the relationship between the cardiovascular system and anxiety. Anxiety disorder usually changes the body's response to stress. This is due to the combination of some physiological and hormonal reactions that help people flee from threat to safety. Anxiety disorder can bring in inappropriate experiences that raise blood pressure, thus disturb the heart rhythm and may cause a heart attack. When the stress response is malfunctioning, one will experience inflammation, which in turn causes damage to artery lining. The result is a stage set up for building coronary plague. Those who experience anxiety have also been found to have low levels of fatty acids and omega 3. Depression and anxiety also have adverse effects on the platelets as they make them stickier and in turn, cause an unnecessary blood clot. Anxiety and depression also have a connection in terms of diagnosis. For example, when one is diagnosed with a heart problem, this may raise their baseline anxiety. To add on that anxious people also sometimes adopt an unhealthy lifestyle as a way to cope. Some of the unhealthy lifestyles may be drinking, and smoking may worsen the risk to their cardiac system. This means that the harmful effects of anxiety should not be ignored at any stage.

Meditation for anxiety helps calm nerves and reduces the potential effect of anxiety. It is more of a control measure that keeps one's anxiety under check. Appreciating the need for meditation is an indirect way of confirming that we value ourselves and bodies and are keen to transform and make changes. Patients should also note that anxiety alone does not cause depression and heart attack. It can only contribute bin some scenarios. However, as we realize our responsibility with regards to our mental health, we need to consider the contributions of professionals and do more research on the subject matter. When one experiences some symptoms for a minor heart attack, it should not be mistaken for an anxiety attack. Be aware of your environment always because there are emotional, psychological, and mental triggers to anxiety. Handle each with care and caution, and do not be afraid to say how you feel. When you feel restless to talk, consider doing some breathing exercises that are discussed in the book below. Also, know and understand that you are not the only one dealing with this problem. It is a common thing that affects millions of people. It can be treated if you have a positive mindset. Also, come up with various ways of coping mechanisms of handling anxiety for a healthier, better life. For all patients who have experienced anxiety, mediation should be a must in your life. Make it a daily routine and let your mind body and soul guide you through the process. Also, there is a need to keep away from unhealthy life habits, which will worsen our health and harm us.

Five Key Meditation Points

Body Position

It is good to be comfortable and relaxed during the meditation process. However, being too comfortable can sometimes make on lazy to meditate or even fall asleep. If you want to sit on the floor, consider sitting on a rug, you can cross your legs and open your palms. Always ensure that you are in an upright position, your back should be straight and do not bend your neck. If you like sitting on a chair, do not sit on a comfortable chair or a couch. Pick an armchair or a study chair and sit upright without straining any muscle. This will ensure that you are comfortable enough to concentrate and not too comfortable to drift off. Body position can also determine whether you follow meditation to the end or you drift off in the process. As useful as sitting in an upright position during the study, meditation to needs the same input. After this, you can slowly start breathing exercises.

Do not worry if your mind wonders of or if you do not concentrate immediately. Meditation is a process; thus, disruptions are meant to happen at one stage or the other. Sitting should not be restricted indoors. If you love nature, you can go to a park or do it in your backyard. Once you set up the place and ready, be sure to maintain the upright and accep0table sitting position. This is also because your full body needs to feel and realize the exercises that you are doing. It is okay to lift you heap up or down if you want to, but your back should be in an upright position. You also appreciate technology and download apps that guide you on the right body position for meditation.

Immerse Yourself in the Present Moment and Ward off Negative Thoughts

Be keen and aware of your present moment. When you first begin meditation exercises, you are guided to learn to work with various elements of distractions. Most distractions are external, for instance, smell, noise, and sounds. Some are internal, for example, thoughts, emotions, and sensations. Always be ready to let go of any distractions before beginning the meditation process. Enabling can be done for a set period depending on how much time has been set up for the meditation. Giving go also helps us keep our focus, which is essential and crucial. Without this kind of intention, however, distractions will pull us out of our meditation without our own free will or consent. When we free ourselves from distractions, it means we are setting ourselves free from perceptions, judgment, and any other concern which can divert our focus on the present moment. Some mediators achieve this by picturing themselves like an empty vessel. This means they are hollow inside with no memory or history of the past. At the beginner stage, one has an open mind and is accepting any outcome whatsoever. They are also not caught up in habitual patterns. During meditation, we do not spend the whole time agonizing of the past and how bad it has been and how unfair life is. We focus on the present moment, how life is enjoyable — ways on how we can have fun and be more productive. We do not take for granted the things that we have. We accept our past mistakes without regrets or blame game. During this moment we want to be happy and will only concentrate on the things that make us happy. It is like living in a life with no regrets and enjoying the things that we have now. It is valuing the present without compromising in the future.

Getting negative thought sometimes is not easy but can be done if you know how. Consider the people who surround you from family, friends, and colleagues. Check on their mindset and view on things. Are they positive in their words or negative and can bring you down? Are they encouraging towards your take on meditation for anxiety? From this, you can design your social cycle and surround yourself with people who help you improve and have your best interest at heart. Having a positive mindset will free you from feeling guilty about doing the things you do. It will also help you learn from your past mistakes and help you move to the future stronger and more resilient. You will also be able to come up with a beneficial coping mechanism to your anxiety and reduce living a stressful life. Spread your positivity across your social cycle and help- other people cope too. By doing this, you will be inspiring many and helping them be the best they can be. Using positive words go a long way in helping people cope with their problems and any issue affecting them. At home, be the role model and spread positivity all over. Chances are others will learn and also strive to be the same. Be in control of your emotions as they also have a direct impact on your anxiety. Simple things should not anger you and do not be like some people who react to the situation. If you encounter any case that is likely to make you anxious, breath in and out, then whisper positive, encouraging words that will make you believe that all will be okay. As you do this, inform that safe person whom you can trust and make them know how you feel. Encourage yourself to be in control and accept the things you cannot change. Be on standby in case of negative feedback and face the consequences with courage. Be ready to move on from all those once all are finished and done with. Chances are you will emerge out with a better and more relaxed mind. Solving issues as they come to help you not keep things that anger you in your heart. Therefore, doing all these are for the betterment of your health and healthy living. It also helps you not to blame yourself for the occurrence of things you had no control over.

The heartbeat and pulse rate can signify how anxious someone is. Be keen on how fast or slow your heart is beating. You can do this by using your left hand to press your wrist. You monitor this before you begin your meditation process. As you breathe in and out and relax a little bit, also monitor the change in your heart bit. Generally, as you experience the relaxation in your mind, the heartbeat gradually drops to a reasonable rate. That is why it is right to say that meditation can be a natural remedy for anxiety and other mental illnesses. It does not require any special tools or equipment. All it needs is a willing and ready heart. Does the soothing music or calm environment calm your heart bit? You need to recognize this since not all who experience calmness have a reduced heartbeat. While some people's music will work, others need a quiet environment, and others still enjoy places they can experience nature at its finest. When your pulse is still fast, do not be hard on yourself. It may signify the fact that you are not relaxed and is still preoccupied with other things. In this scenario, you can consider changing the setting or location then starting over again. It is not a crime to start over again since some configuration can be a bit destructive than others. Reasonable pulse rate usually signifies that everything is working normally.

Display Pleasant Imagery

There is a crucial meditation aspect that is focused on settling on a single object of focus. There are different objects that you can focus on, which include but not limited to a candle flame, your breath, mantra or chant, and physical sensations. Most people use the breath to form good images in their minds. This helps them maintain their focus and realize an effective meditation routine. Concentrating on a specific thing helps one let go of distractions and gladly embrace the current moment. If you have positive experiences, they can as well help build the balance of letting go of all the negativity. As you focus on the meditation object, the mind will get rid of all the jumpy distractions, which may give rise to more stress and anxiety. Pleasant imagery also brings about happy feelings and ignites positive feelings that form relaxation. If you are satisfied with what you see, chances are you will be less distracted and stay more focused on what you are doing. You do not need to feel that you have to stick with one image. You can alternate daily, and the advantage of this is a different image illicit different memory, thus creates all-round healing. As you get used to meditation exercises, however, you will realize that there is one particular image that you are fond of. Feel free to use it more frequently.

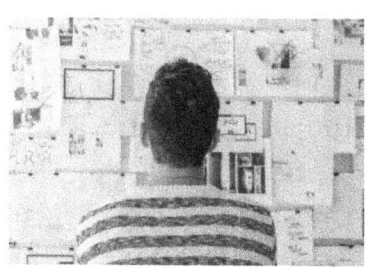

Activate All the Senses

Ensure that all your feelings are active during the meditation process. The sense of smell can bring sweet aroma, which ignites the memory of your favorite childhood meal. The ascent of the rose flower may bring about consciousness of the best garden you have ever been to. A sense of vision can be active during the imagery of the candle. By glazing at the candle burning, one can free distractions from their mind and concentrate more. A sense of touch will be significant when you are feeling your pulse rate and holding your chest as you inhale and exhale. If all senses are active, then you will handle all the meditation exercises in your full self and realize deep inner healing.

The choice of treating anxiety through meditation is determined by an individual concerned. This is because it requires dedication and commitment. It should not be forced, but the victim needs to understand and realize that they are doing it for their good. Young people are often aware of their heartbeat to the extent that it makes some of them anxious. However, studies have shown that as you age, the constant awareness diminishes.

Chapter 12: Benefits Of Meditation

The popularity of meditation is increasing as more people discover its benefits.

You can use it to increase awareness of yourself and your surroundings. Many people think of it as a way to reduce stress and develop concentration.

People also use the practice to develop other beneficial habits and feelings, such as a positive mood and outlook, self-discipline, healthy sleep patterns and even increased pain tolerance.

Here are the benefits of meditation:

Improves Sleep

Nearly half the population will struggle with insomnia at some point.

One study compared two mindfulness-based meditation programs by randomly assigning participants to one of two groups. One group practiced meditation, while the other didn't.

Participants who meditated fell asleep sooner and stayed asleep longer, compared to those who didn't meditate.

Becoming skilled in meditation may help you control or redirect the racing or "runaway" thoughts that often lead to insomnia.

Additionally, it can help relax your body, releasing tension and placing you in a peaceful state in which you're more likely to fall asleep.

Greater Sense of Self-Awareness

Meditation allows us to mentally take inventory of our bodies. How does our body feel in the present moment? What amazing things is our body capable of? Do we feel strong or weak? What can we do to remedy anything that aches in our body?

Much like the physical practice of yoga, meditation helps you establish a stronger connection between mind and body. Through this greater sense of self-awareness, we cultivate present moment awareness which allows us to remain present, grounded, and focused in all aspects and every moment of our lives.

Meditation Can Help with Addiction

A growing number of studies has shown that, given its effects on the self-control regions of the brain, meditation can be very effective in helping people recover from various types of addiction. One study, for example, pitted mindfulness training against the American Lung Association's freedom from smoking (FFS) program, and found that people who learned mindfulness were many times more likely to have quit smoking by the end of the training, and at 17 weeks follow-up, than those in the conventional treatment. This may be because meditation helps people "decouple" the state of craving from the act of smoking, so the one doesn't always have to lead to the other, but rather you fully experience and ride out the "wave" of craving, until it passes. Other research has found that mindfulness training, mindfulness-based cognitive therapy (MBCT), and mindfulness-based relapse prevention (MBRP) can be helpful in treating other forms of addiction.

Reduces Stress

Stress reduction is one of the most common reasons people try meditation.

One study including over 3,500 adults showed that it lives up to its reputation for stress reduction.

Normally, mental and physical stress cause increased levels of the stress hormone cortisol. This produces many of the harmful effects of stress, such as the release of inflammation-promoting chemicals called cytokines.

These effects can disrupt sleep, promote depression and anxiety, increase blood pressure and contribute to fatigue and cloudy thinking.

In an eight-week study, a meditation style called "mindfulness meditation" reduced the inflammation response caused by stress.

Another study in nearly 1,300 adults demonstrated that meditation may decrease stress. Notably, this effect was strongest in individuals with the highest levels of stress.

Research has shown that meditation may also improve symptoms of stress-related conditions, including irritable bowel syndrome, post-traumatic stress disorder and fibromyalgia

Short Meditation Breaks Can Help Kids in School

For developing brains, meditation has as much as or perhaps even more promise than it has for adults. There's been increasing interest from educators and researchers in bringing meditation and yoga to school kids, who are dealing with the usual stressors inside school, and oftentimes additional stress and trauma outside school. Some schools have started implementing meditation into their daily schedules, and with good effect: One district in San Francisco started a twice daily meditation program in some of its high-risk schools – and saw suspensions decrease, and GPAs and attendance increase. Studies have confirmed the cognitive and emotional benefits of meditation for schoolchildren, but more work will probably need to be done before it gains more widespread acceptance.

You Can Meditate Anywhere

People practice many different forms of meditation, most of which don't require specialized equipment or space. You can practice with just a few minutes daily.

If you want to start meditating, try choosing a form of meditation based on what you want to get out of it.

There are two major styles of meditation:

Focused-attention meditation: Concentrates attention on a single object, thought, sound or visualization. It emphasizes ridding your mind of attention and distraction. Meditation may focus on breathing, a mantra or a calming sound.

Open-monitoring meditation: Encourages broadened awareness of all aspects of your environment, train of thought and sense of self. It may include becoming aware of thoughts, feelings or impulses that you might normally try to suppress.

Controls Anxiety

Obsessing about the past or future can often lead to unhappiness. When we are fully immersed in the present moment, we are content. We can only control what's happening now – which is why there is no reason to be caught up in the past or fixate on the future.

Our life is always in the now. Meditation is the anchor to help you stay there. This is the key to reducing stress, gaining control over your anxiety.

Increase Mental Clarity and Focus

If we are mindful and focused on the present moment, we are fully engaged in present action. Think of how amazing all your work would be if you were completely focused on it, and not caught up in the chatter of your mind, or impulsively checking your cell phone or social media every five minutes.

Meditation helps us unplug and tune in to what's going on beneath the surface of our thoughts. Over time, this becomes a subconscious habit that results in increased mental clarity and focus, and your memory and mental acuity will improve too.

Meditation Reduces Activity in the Brain's "Me Center"

One of the most interesting studies in the last few years, carried out at Yale

University, found that mindfulness meditation decreases activity in the default mode network (DMN), the brain network responsible for mind-wandering and self-referential thoughts – a.k.a., "monkey mind." The DMN is "on" or active when we're not thinking about anything in particular, when our minds are just wandering from thought to thought. Since mind-wandering is typically associated with being less happy, ruminating, and worrying about the past and future, it's the goal for many people to dial it down. Several studies have shown that meditation, through its quieting effect on the DMN, appears to do just this. And even when the mind does start to wander, because of the new connections that form, meditators are better at snapping back out of it.

Promotes Emotional Health

Some forms of meditation can also lead to an improved self-image and more positive outlook on life.

Two studies of mindfulness meditation found decreased depression in over 4,600 adults.

One study followed 18 volunteers as they practiced meditation over three years. The study found that participants experienced long-term decreases in depression.

Inflammatory chemicals called cytokines, which are released in response to stress, can affect mood, leading to depression. A review of several studies suggests meditation may reduce depression by decreasing these inflammatory chemicals.

Another controlled study compared electrical activity between the brains of people who practiced mindfulness meditation and the brains of others who did not.

Those who meditated showed measurable changes in activity in areas related to positive thinking and optimism

Emotional Intelligence

When we have time to sit without any distractions, we are able to get more in touch with our emotions. We may realize the root cause of our unrest or worry.

Regular meditation helps us recognize our emotions as fleeting, but also allows us the chance to sit with them instead of avoiding or being afraid of facing our emotions.

Through the ability to sit with your thoughts, you can work through emotions instead of continuing to ignore or repress them. As a result, you deepen your emotional intelligence and ability to recognize and work through emotional issues as they arise, which impacts your relationships and mind state in a positive way.

Meditation May Lead to Volume Changes in Key Areas of the Brain

In 2011, Sara Lazar and her team at Harvard found that mindfulness meditation can actually change the structure of the brain: Eight weeks of Mindfulness-Based Stress Reduction (MBSR) was found to increase cortical thickness in the hippocampus, which governs learning and memory, and in certain areas of the brain that play roles in emotion regulation and self-referential processing. There were also decreases in brain cell volume in the amygdala, which is responsible for fear, anxiety, and stress – and these changes matched the participants' self-reports of their stress levels, indicating that meditation not only changes the brain, but it changes our subjective perception and feelings as well. In fact, a follow-up study by Lazar's team found that after meditation training, changes in brain areas linked to mood and arousal were also linked to improvements in how participants said they felt — i.e., their psychological well-being. So for anyone who says that activated blobs in the brain don't necessarily mean anything, our subjective experience – improved mood and well-being – does indeed seem to be shifted through meditation as well.

Triggers the Brain's Relaxation Response

According to Herbert Benson, founder of the Mind-Body Medical Institute, meditation ignites the 'relaxation response' in the brain. Components of this response include changes in heart rate, metabolism and brain chemistry, all in the name of bringing you – and your brain – to a heightened state of relaxation.

Sounds wonderful, doesn't it?! It is! And this relaxation can lead to better sleep, falling asleep quicker, and also stress management, reduced anxiety and a better ability to maintain emotional equilibrium.

Just a Few Days of Training Improves Concentration and Attention

Having problems concentrating isn't just a kid thing – it affects millions of grown-ups as well, with an ADD diagnosis or not. Interestingly but not surprisingly, one of the central benefits of meditation is that it improves attention and concentration: One recent study found that just a couple of weeks of meditation training helped people's focus and memory during the verbal reasoning section of the GRE. In fact, the increase in score was equivalent to 16 percentile points, which is nothing to sneeze at. Since the strong focus of attention (on an object, idea, or activity) is one of the central aims of meditation, it's not so surprising that meditation should help people's cognitive skills on the job, too – but it's nice to have science confirm it. And everyone can use a little extra assistance on standardized tests.

Lengthens Attention Span

Focused-attention meditation is like weight lifting for your attention span. It helps increase the strength and endurance of your attention.

For example, a study looked at the effects of an eight-week mindfulness meditation course and found it improved participants' ability to reorient and maintain their attention.

A similar study showed that human resource workers who regularly practiced mindfulness meditation stayed focused on a task for longer.

These workers also remembered details of their tasks better than their peers who did not practice meditation.

Moreover, one review concluded that meditation may even reverse patterns in the brain that contribute to mind-wandering, worrying and poor attention.

Even meditating for a short period may benefit you. One study found that four days of practicing meditation may be enough to increase attention span.

How Can Meditation Practice Help During Pregnancy?

The endocrine system undergoes a massive spike during pregnancy, and the effect lingers for a few months after delivery. Pregnant women often find it challenging to cope with their emotions or talk about it.

Despite being aware of the unreasonableness, they fail to control the automatic thoughts and get overwhelmed by the recurrent mood fluctuations. Work-life balance and personal happiness start going downhill.

Expecting mothers can go through peaceful and positive pregnancy by being mindful from the very beginning. In her book, she urges mothers to "Feel the baby in belly, feel the breath as the belly rises and falls, and just be present with your baby."

Meditation and mindfulness promote a healthy pregnancy and early parenthood like nothing else. Here are some of the positive impacts of meditation for pregnant women that you might be intrigued to know:

Some pilot studies indicate that daily meditation during pregnancy helps would-be mothers maintain a greater connection to their body. By eliminating stress and reducing the fear of labor pain, meditation allows women to stay calmer during delivery and prevent them from experiencing postpartum depression.

Meditation means quality 'me-time,' which many women fail to give themselves. Especially working mothers who are expecting a child, spending some minutes for themselves in between work and daily errands may be a far-reached goal. Cultivating the habit of daily practice cools down the nerves and reduce the tension, which can significantly benefit the health of an expecting mother.

Mood agitations and crankiness during pregnancy can be overwhelming for both the mother and people around her. Meditation calms the mind and regulates mood by controlling disruptive hormones. So, it is the whole family that benefits from self-awareness, not just the person who practices it.

Are there Scientifically Proven Benefits for the Skin?

Our skin is a great communicator of our feelings and mental state. It mirrors extreme emotions such as stress, anxiety, depression, excitement, and happiness, and has a unique way of responding to pressure. For example, our cheeks turn pink as we blush, and our ears feel hot and red when we feel embarrassed and humiliated.

Fear makes the skin look pale, and sadness can often bring dullness and unwanted crinkles in the skin. Together with blood circulation and hormonal ups and downs, the skin is an excellent indicator of our emotions and science has gone an extra mile proving it.

Recent research by Dr. Anthony Bewley, a popular dermatologist, proved that self-healing practices like meditation, breath control, and mindfulness, have profound benefits on skin conditions like eczema, acne, dry skin, and psoriasis.

This branch of study, popularly called psychodermatology, explores how the skin reacts to internal stress and how stress-reduction through meditation impacts it. Some studies revealed that when individuals with psoriasis attended guided meditation sessions or listened to soothing pieces of music, they healed a lot faster than others with the same condition.

Besides the direct impact, meditation also adds glow and youthfulness to the skin by curing allied health conditions. For example, gastric ulcers, insomnia, regular headache or migraine, hypertension or low blood pressure, and chronic pain are common issues that negatively reflect on our skin tone.

Daily meditation helps in reducing these anomalies and subsequently helps in slowing down the aging process of the skin, making us look younger and brighter naturally.

Chapter 13: Introduction To Meditation

Most people believe that meditation is synonymous to breathing in yoga. But, meditation is more than that. Through meditation, you can learn to focus. You can train your mind and rewire the electrical circuits to ensure that you develop skills and strengths that you require to solve problems. There are different types of meditation that you can follow to help you achieve your goals. The different types of meditation are covered later in the book.

The techniques mentioned and taught in this book will help you reduce stress. These techniques will help you focus on the present and not on the emotions or thoughts that drive you. You will also learn to control some reactions to stress. You must remember that the stress that you face is limiting your happiness. You are often stressed because you believe that you are not happy with where you are in your life. There are many people who constantly work because they want to amass enough wealth to support their family. But, do you think they lead a happy life? Do you think they spend time with their kids? The answer to both these questions is no. They only believe they are happy.

If you lead such a life, you should practice meditation since it will help you identify your priorities. You can uncover the mysteries of your mind and see why your mind does what it does to help you stay happy. You will also understand how to overcome such efforts. Only when you identify this will you be able to attain genuine happiness. This is the happiness that never lets you down and never changes. You can be confident that this happiness will last for a very long time.

Through meditation, you will learn that you can genuinely be happy. You will learn that you do not have to resort to temporary happiness. You will learn to train your mind to find happiness within yourself and not in an outside person or power.

The goal of meditation is to remove stress and to keep you happy. You will develop qualities like honesty, compassion, integrity, and mindfulness, and will learn that happiness comes from within you. It does not require the affirmation of another person. Meditation is hence a practice that helps in spreading happiness and kindness within you and within people around you.

When you begin to meditate, you learn how to de-stress. When you are calm, you will learn to maintain your temper and will stop depending on people to help you solve your problems. When you are under stress, you place an extra burden on yourself and on the people around you, which affects your relationships. But when your mind learns how to stop causing stress, you will find yourself in a position where you can help yourself and others. Hence, through the practice of meditation, you will learn to respect yourself for the things that you are worthy of. You will find that your desire to gain happiness does not harm you or the society around you.

You will be able to find happiness for yourself on your own.

Myths About Meditation

Meditation is only about Concentration

Meditation is not concentration. When you meditate, you learn to focus better on the tasks at hand. Unlike concentration, meditation is a relaxation technique and does not require any effort. You learn to let go of your emotions and thoughts and find yourself in a state of deep relaxation. It is, therefore, easier for you to concentrate.

Meditation is a Religious Practice

Meditation and yoga transcend every religion since they are ancient practices. There is no criterion as to which religion can meditate and which cannot. Meditation can probably bring faiths, nations and countries together. Meditation benefits every human being on the planet. 'Gurudev' Sri Sri Ravi Shankar once said that he would like to encourage people from all backgrounds to meditate.

Always Sit in the Lotus Posture When You Meditate

A scientific study called the 'Patanjali Yoga Sutras' unravels the nature of the human mind. The study says that people must be steady and comfortable when they meditate since it enhances their experience. You can either sit cross-legged on a chair or sofa. You can also stand if that makes you feel better. You only need to ensure that your back is straight.

Only Old People should Meditate

Meditation adds value to people of any age group. You can start meditating at the age of ten. Meditation is synonymous to a shower, in the sense that it helps to keep your mind stress-free and clear, just how a shower keeps your body clean.

Meditation is like Hypnotism

Meditation is a medicine for hypnosis. When a person is hypnotized, he or she is not aware of what they are doing. Meditation is about being aware of every moment in your life. While hypnotism makes a person believe in the impressions in their mind, meditation helps to free the person from those impressions. It helps to clear their consciousness. While hypnotism increases metabolic activity, meditation decreases it.

Meditation Controls Your Thoughts

People do not invite their thoughts. They are aware of their thoughts only when they pass through your mind. A thought is like the clouds in the sky: they come when they want to and go away on their own. If you want to control your thoughts, you must make extra effort. When you meditate, you do not allow your mind to dwell on the positive thoughts or reject the negative thoughts. You only witness your thoughts and move them into a silent space within your mind.

Meditation Helps You Run Away from Problems

Meditation helps to empower people to face their problems with a smile. Through meditation, one can develop the skills to handle any situation in a constructive and pleasant manner. You can learn to accept a situation for what it is and then make a conscious effort to work on that situation. You will stop worrying about the future and forget the past. When you meditate regularly, you will find that you have better self-esteem and have the strength to take up new challenges. Meditation will help you move ahead in life with confidence.

You Must Meditate for Hours to Experience Bliss

People do not have to sit down for hours to enhance their experience. You can establish a connection with your source in a fraction of a second. If you meditate for at least twenty minutes each and every day, you will develop a strong connection with your inner self. The quality of your meditation will also improve and you will experience the benefits of meditation.

You will become a Recluse or a Monk if You Meditate

It is not necessary for one to give up their material life if they want to lead a spiritual life. When you meditate, the quality of your life improves and you learn to appreciate the little things in life. You can be happy and keep the people around you happy when you have a peaceful and relaxed mind.

You should Face Certain Directions and only Meditate at Certain Times

You can meditate whenever you want to and face any direction when you want to meditate. You should keep in mind that your stomach should not be full. Otherwise, you will doze off immediately. It is a good practice to meditate either at sunrise or sunset since it can help to keep you energetic and calm throughout the day.

I hope this chapter has helped to remove your inhibitions about meditation. Now that you have a better idea of what meditation truly is, let us look at the benefits of meditation.

Conclusion

Meditation, relaxation, and getting ahold of your anxiety and stresses are so essential that lots of people don't even realize that they're in this situation. Anxiety can't always entirely go away, but you should realize that you're the one who is at cause here and the one who is going to change the state of your life.

You owe it to yourself to control the outcome from each and every single interaction, and by making the correct decisions, and working towards a better, more fulfilling life, you'll be happier as well, and meditation can majorly help with this it's an excellent way to practice just general relaxation and even just a few small changes can make a huge difference.

So yes, start to make the change that you want to make. If you feel like you just can't relax, then you should take some time and work on trying to be a better, happier person in life. If you're working to improve yourself, then let meditation be that guiding force that can help you do what you feel you need to do. Whether you're new to it or not, or if you've done a meditation once or many times, use these to help improve your general life, and to make you better than ever.

Relaxation doesn't have to be something you can't ever obtain, nor does it have to be something that's a pipe dream, for, with a few changes, you can start to live a more relaxed, happier life.

www.ingramcontent.com/pod-product-compliance
Lightning Source LLC
Chambersburg PA
CBHW071837080526
44589CB00012B/1030